Knowing God Is Knowing Love

May your faith always be a beautiful witness of Divine Love in the world,

Many Blessings
Linda F. Stafford

LINDA F. STAFFORD

To God Be The Glory!

ISBN 978-1-64028-522-4 (paperback)
ISBN 978-1-64028-523-1 (digital)

Copyright © 2017 by Linda F. Stafford

All rights reserved. No part of this publication may be reproduced, distributed, or transmitted in any form or by any means, including photocopying, recording, or other electronic or mechanical methods without the prior written permission of the publisher. For permission requests, solicit the publisher via the address below.

Christian Faith Publishing, Inc.
832 Park Avenue
Meadville, PA 16335
www.christianfaithpublishing.com

Printed in the United States of America

How does one write a book about knowing God? For me, it began with just one word or phrase chosen one day at a time from my morning devotional readings. I used that one word or phrase as my mantra (my sacred counsel). The word given me by the Holy Spirit always guided and helped me react to each situation that arose during the day.

> "Let the morning bring me <u>word</u> of your unfailing love, for I have put my trust in you. Show me the way I should go, for to you I lift up my soul" (Ps. 143:8).

At the end of each month, I lit a candle, said a prayer, and with pen in hand, I let the Holy Spirit guide what was written concerning each daily word. What follows is what was written from the Holy Spirit through my listening heart. The spirit has moved me to share the collection of the journals that have accumulated over the years and to let this be a positive experience.

One of the things I have come to understand and appreciate is that God always journeys with us. There will be days of darkness in our life but God brings light. He is present and I trust in him.

> "I trust in the Lord; my soul trusts in his <u>word</u>. My soul waits for the Lord more than sentinels wait for the dawn" (Ps. 130:5–6).

Coming to know God is a lifelong journey. The wonderful, marvelous truth is that he has always known and loved us.

> *"O Lord, you have probed me and you know me; you know when I sit and when I stand; you understand my thoughts from afar. My journeys and my rest you scrutinize, with all my ways you are familiar. Even before a <u>word</u> is on my tongue, behold, O Lord, you know the whole of it. Behind me and before, you hem me in and rest your hand upon me. Such knowledge is too wonderful for me; too lofty for me to attain . . . verse 13-14 truly you have formed my inmost being; you knit me in my mother's womb. I give you thanks that I am fearfully, wonderfully made; wonderful are your works" (Ps. 139:1–6).*

We are people on a journey. Many times we just don't know what we are searching for. The answer lies in a more focused commitment to God and to each other. Each of us has to find our way to a deeper relationship with the source of life. Our own unique way to prayer, reading scripture, and reflecting more on what is important to us. God always journeys with us. The best we can do is to choose to open our hearts to the love he has for us. No one else can make this choice for us. Although it is a personal choice, we still need each other's love, support, and prayers.

We come to know the Lord through each other. We do make a difference in each other's lives. When we open our hearts to Jesus, follow where he leads, and allow his presence to shine through us, our relationships become more loving and gentle.

> *"And we, who with unveiled faces all reflect the Lord's glory, are being transformed into his likeness with ever-increasing glory which comes from the Lord, which is the Spirit" (2 Cor. 3:18).*

Praying together enhances and ennobles us. Any touch of beauty is a God touch. The greatest God touches are those experiences of loving and being loved. Successful living requires that we recognize the gifts that we are in other's lives. We need to accept the truth that others need us, and that we need them.

We must listen carefully to what we read and to what people of faith have to say. In turn, we speak from our hearts with *words* of encouragement, hope, and faith. We all pray for the grace to come to know and to have a deeper love for God revealed in Jesus, a God who is "slow to anger, rich in kindness, and a God of infinite love."

My life word is "love." Love will lift you higher than anything. Love will also bring you to your knees. We are to live with faith, hope, and love. God's *word* teaches us that the greatest of these is *love*.

I encourage you to start your day with God in prayer and reflective reading. A good place to start is with the Bible.

"In the beginning was the Word, and the Word was with God, and the Word was God. He was in the beginning with God. All things came to be through him, and without him nothing came to be. What came to be through him was life, and this life was the light of the human race; the light shines in the darkness, and the darkness has not overcome it" (John 1:1–5).

Yes, God's *Word* was made flesh and He does dwell among us. God's marvelous plan of salvation is for you and for me. God's plan is for all of us to walk together allowing his light to help us.

Begin your journey by selecting one word or phrase for the day and let the rest of the day be a reflection of your prayer time. Let the one word support your thoughts and deeds. If we don't let God in, we are apt to be on the wrong track all day. When we open our hearts to the Lord, everything we do will be marked with the presence of God.

"Thy Word is a lamp unto my feet and a light unto my path" (Ps. 119:105).

My journey is in the following pages. The list begins with the word or phrase chosen at the beginning of the day and is then the combined words for my monthly reflection. For me it was like using and following a recipe. I also pray for you as Paul prayed for the Ephesians.

> *"I pray that out of his glorious riches he may strengthen you with power through his Spirit in your inner being, so that Christ may dwell in your hearts through faith. And I pray that you, being rooted and established in love, may have power, together with all the saints, to grasp how wide and long and high and deep is the love of Christ, and to know this love that surpasses knowledge—that you may be filled to the measure of all the fullness of God" (Eph. 3:16–19).*

Enjoy your journey.

2005

Words for January 2005

1. Time
2. Angels
3. Faith
4. Spark
5. Thanks
6. Rest
7. Humor
8. Alone
9. Light
10. Opening
11. Understanding
12. Heartsick
13. Joyful
14. Share
15. Bless
16. Holy Spirit
17. Friends
18. Risk
19. Hope
20. Delight
21. Comforted
22. Healing
23. Thanksgiving
24. Peace
25. Wait
26. Gift
27. Journey
28. Planning
29. Good
30. Tenderness
31. Continuous
32. Grateful
33. Concern
34. Angels
35. Sustain
36. Trust
37. Littleness
38. Love
39. Guidance
40. Thirst
41. Saved
42. Fidelity
43. Calm
44. Courage
45. Worship
46. Kindness
47. Time
48. Rest
49. Relax
50. Guided
51. Silence
52. Faith
53. Goodness
54. Love
55. Cherish
56. Grace
57. Joy
58. Great
59. Time
60. Calm

61. Listen
62. Respect
63. All is well
64. Bless
65. Divine Mercy
66. Treasures
67. Compassion
68. Praise
69. Hospitality.

January 2005: *"For I will give you words and a wisdom that none of your opponents will be able to withstand or contradict" (Lk. 21:15).*

End of month reflections for January 2005

It is time to trust the angels. Faith in God is a beautiful gift. Let the Holy Spirit spark thankfulness and guide you to a much-needed rest. Gentle humor will return to your soul.

Spending time alone helps you to see the light. It opens you to a deeper level of understanding. If you are heartsick and feeling no joy, share your emotions. Share the blessings of the Holy Spirit with your friends. Dare to risk in the hope that brings delight in the joys of friendships when you share the love in your heart.

Let yourself be comforted by God's healing love with thanksgiving for the peace in your soul. Keep loving as you wait patiently for the many gifts you will receive on this journey called life. Keep planning good memories. Show tenderness with a grateful heart and deep concern for others. Angels will guide you.

Sustain loving relationships. Trust in their love. Don't let littleness guide your thoughts. Love God, love others. Let yourself be loved by loving yourself. Seek guidance when in doubt, thirst after righteousness. We are saved by grace.

Trust in God's fidelity. Be calm with great courage when troubles come. Worship God all the days of your life. Show kindness to yourself by taking quiet time to rest and relax in God's presence. Be guided by the Holy Spirit. Let peaceful silence feel your empty space. Faith grows in stillness. Goodness is a great gift from God. Love and cherish your loved ones. Cherish the moments of love that are freely given.

KNOWING GOD IS KNOWING LOVE

"Above all, love each other deeply, because love covers a multitude of sins" (1 Pet. 4:8).

God's grace brings great joy. Time calms any storm. Listen to your heart, to the very depth of your being. Respect that deep, inner feeling. Don't do anything contrary to that because the Holy Spirit is leading you.

Yes, all is well. God has blessed us. All that God blesses is for our good. Through God's Divine Mercy, treasures abound. In God's great compassion, he is always there for us when we are hurting. Guardian of our soul! We are called to have compassion (to suffer with, to get involved with others in their suffering). We are called to praise God in all things. We are called to show hospitality when needed.

Words for February 2005

1. Solitude and silence
2. The light of love
3. Be not afraid
4. Honor
5. Gentle humor
6. Rejoice
7. Wait
8. Little thing count
9. Strength
10. Deepest
11. Faithfulness
12. Forgive
13. Enjoy
14. Peace
15. Love
16. God's presence
17. Patient
18. Laugh
19. Humble
20. Delight
21. Joy
22. Mercy
23. Reflect
24. Loving kindness
25. Respect
26. Spirit
27. Listen
28. Love.

February 2005: *"Come away by yourself to a deserted place and rest a while" (Mk. 6:31).*

End of month reflections for February 2005

Solitude and silence, peace and quiet are opportunities for healing and growth. These help to bring the light of God's love into your life. Do not be afraid of the quiet. Honor your alone time. Be gentle in humor when it involves others. Do right by the people in your life. Rejoice by letting the light of God's loving presence shine on all you do. Wait on God to show you the way.

When it comes to doing something for someone, remember that little things count. Little things help give strength to the deepest part in faithful friendships. Be willing to forgive shortcomings so you can return to enjoy life shared. Be at peace with yourself and with others.

Joys come every day through God's loving presence. Be patient with all. Laugh a lot. Humbly delight in other's joys and accomplishments. Let Divine Mercy reflect God's loving kindness to your very soul. Have a great respect for the spirit of the Living God. Listen to him with great love. Care enough to care.

Words for March 2005

1. Tenderness
2. Light
3. Comfort
4. Joy
5. Value
6. Rejoice
7. Wisdom
8. Reflect kindness
9. Peace
10. Abundant goodness
11. Do good
12. Truth
13. Faithfully
14. Believe
15. Simply love
16. Jesus
17. Silence
18. Deep faith
19. Friendship
20. Peace
21. All is well
22. Wait
23. Sincerity
24. Obedience
25. Faith
26. Listen
27. Calm
28. Trust
29. Mercy
30. Goodness.

"Is it true? Is it kind? Is it necessary? This humbling threefold test shows me when I am being untruthful, unkind, unfair" (Laura Ingalls Wilder)

End of month reflections for March 2005

When you show tenderness to others, you radiate a light that shines. A light that brings comfort and joy to the lives of those you encounter. Step out of the shadows; let God's light shine in your life.

Rejoice in the tenderness, the wit and wisdom that are a gift from the Great Giver of all gifts.

Reflect kindness so you can be at peace in all things. There is an abundance of goodness in this world. Set goodness in motion flowing in and out of your life. Faithfully believe in truth. Truth does set you free.

Life is not as difficult as we sometimes make it out to be. All we need to do is simply love, love as Jesus loves. When trouble comes, say the name of Jesus. Remain silent for a time. Let your deep faith take hold. Be true to the friendship you have with Jesus. He will bring peace and wellness to your soul.

Time brings healing. Wait in God's presence. When dealing with other people's pain, have sincerity of heart. Keep your faith strong. Be obedient to God's commands. Listen with a calmness of spirit. Trust in the mercy of God's goodness.

"For now we see only a reflection in a mirror; then we shall see face to face. Now I know in part; then I shall know fully, even as I am fully known" (1 Cor. 13:12, NIV).

Words for April 2005

1. Trust
2. Blessings
3. Giving Spirit
4. Forgiveness
5. Unity
6. Open
7. Courage
8. Sharing
9. Strength
10. Open
11. Believe
12. Faithfulness
13. Divine gift
14. Presence
15. Calm
16. Love
17. Guide
18. Knowing
19. Spirit
20. Joy
21. Time

22. Healing
23. Feeling
24. Simple
25. Rest
26. Rest
27. Joy
28. Lead
29. Sunshine
30. Do right.

End of month reflections for April 2005

Trust in the blessings that are headed your way. Create a giving spirit of mercy, forgiveness, and love (to yourself and to others.)

Create a sense of unity by being open to new ideas. Have the courage to let go of selfishness. Sharing friendships give strength and beauty to your life. Be open to seeing their gifts. Believe in the faithfulness of friendships, knowing these are divine gifts with the light of God's presence.

Keep calm, letting love guide. Knowing God's love helps you to share his love. Have a spirit of joy time after time because joy has a healing affect. Take time to simply rest. Rest brings healing and joy. Lead yourself into God's healing sunshine and to the rest needed for the ability to do what is right for your life.

Words for May 2005

1. Truth
2. Hospitality
3. Comfort
4. Sharing
5. See
6. Gladness
7. Presence
8. Be
9. Slow down
10. Mercy
11. Confess
12. All is well
13. Praise
14. Delight
15. Tenderness
16. Joy
17. Confidence
18. Wisdom
19. Trust
20. Surrender
21. Little is much
22. Friendship
23. Thankfulness
24. Joyful
25. Love
26. Faith
27. Peace of Christ
28. Humble
29. Presence
30. Praise
31. Humble.

End of month reflections for May 2005

The truth is, humbly, I need you, Lord. I need your tenderness and comfort. I confess, it is your presence I seek. Be merciful to me as I rush from task to task. Teach me the value of slowing down, surrendering my love, my friendships, my praise to your divine presence.

In this praise time, I humbly realize that all is well, that little is much, and that I can have a joyful confidence as I trust in your great wisdom to guide me on my faith journey.

When I take the time to offer you hospitality in my heart with thankfulness for the joy of the peace of Christ, it is then that I can truly delight in your presence and love. As gladness feels my whole being, I am able to once again share my humble faith and lift my heart in praise.

Words for June 2005

1. Joy
2. Live life
3. Love
4. Courage
5. Tenderness
6. Prayer
7. Calm
8. Gift
9. Faith
10. Patience
11. A listening heart
12. Be watchful
13. Finding
14. Guide
15. Inspire
16. Courage
17. Tenderly
18. Commitment
19. Praise
20. Miracles
21. Bless
22. Faithful
23. Treasure
24. Duty
25. Friendship
26. Gratitude
27. Blessed
28. Kindness
29. Good
30. Peace.

End of month reflections for June 2005

Start with joy in the morning. Then live life all day long with love, courage, and tenderness. Prayer is the key to keeping calm in the little and/or big things that pop up during the day. Remember the gift of life. Be thankful for the gift of faith. Patience is tried but can be won.

Listen to people with your heart. Be watchful for the goodness inside you and in others. Finding goodness is the goal. Seek guidance from faithful believers. Inspire others as we journey together. Take courage when having a bad day. Be tender, as Jesus is tender. Remember your commitment to do right. Praise the efforts of others. Praise God, miracles still happen. Open your eyes, bless and be blessed. Remain faithful, treasuring friendships. Do your duty, faithfully in your work and in relationships. Show gratitude, kindness, and a peaceful spirit for the good in your life. Be at peace.

Words for July 2005

1. Shine
2. Pray
3. Simple
4. Freedom
5. Play
6. Patience
7. Joy
8. Guide
9. Faith
10. Honesty
11. Guardian Angels
12. Strength
13. Good
14. Protected
15. Sharing
16. Laughter
17. Be still
18. Know
19. Believe
20. Do right
21. Thankfulness and praise
22. Shine
23. Peace
24. Seekers
25. God guided
26. Silent
27. Seeker
28. Love
29. Trust
30. Listen.

End of month reflections for July 2005

Arise, shine for the glory of the Lord is upon you! Keep prayer simple. Enjoy the freedom of playfulness. Have patience with yourself and with others. Show joy in your smile. Be a guide to others through your deep faith. Seek honesty in all you do. Guardian angels will protect and guide you. Just be open. Strength will come when you need it most. Good things are happening in the world around you. You are protected. Keep sharing your love and wealth.

Laughter is indeed a good medicine. Be still and know God. Believe and do what is right. Have a special spirit of thankfulness and praise. Let your light shine. Be at peace with yourself. Be a seeker of truth. God will guide you. Learn to be silent when you don't have anything good to say. Be seekers of goodness and love. Trust and listen close to your instincts. Have a spirit of gratitude.

Same words combined again.

Arise, shine after you pray. It is simple prayer that releases a special freedom allowing you to play as a child of God. Have patience. The joy will come again. As a little child guided by faith, believe in your guardian angels strength to protect. Know the good of being protected as you share in angelic laughter. Take time to just be still. Know what you believe and do right. Have a spirit of thankfulness and praise to the one who helps you. Realize how much you shine just by having a spirit of peace. Be seekers of a God guided life. Learn when it is best to be silent. Be seekers of his love. Trust God, he is so good and loving. Have a spirit of gratitude and appreciation.

Words for August 2005

1. Faithful
2. Grace
3. Silent
4. Safety
5. Remember
6. Cherish
7. Silence
8. Supply
9. Wisdom
10. Honor
11. Give
12. Privilege
13. Honesty
14. Prayer
15. Simple Rest
16. Sunshine
17. Guidance
18. Acceptance
19. Meek
20. Acceptance
21. Bless
22. Grateful
23. Jesus
24. Tender
25. Kindness/prepare
26. Trust
27. Friend
28. Faith
29. Give
30. To know.

End of month reflections for August 2005

Be faithful to God, yourself, to your church, your family, friends, and job. God's grace will help, just ask. Be silent before God. Let God embrace you in safety. Cherish the love you are given. Learn the gift of silence. God will supply more wisdom and honor when you learn silence (when to keep your mouth shut).

Give away the clutter. It is a privilege to give. Honestly give away what you do not need or want. Simple, honest prayer is the key. Take time to rest in God's presence. His Son will shine on you, giving you guidance and acceptance of the things you cannot change. Meek acceptance of what you cannot change. If you bless, blessing will flow back. Have a grateful heart. Be like Jesus. Be tender, showing kindness will prepare the way for trust. Your best friend is the Lord. Keep the faith. Give from the heart. Know him, the greatest giver. *Intimacy = in-to-me-see.*

Words for September 2005

1. New
2. Grateful Spirit
3. Protected
4. Love
5. Rest
6. Understand
7. Safe
8. God/love
9. Be present
10. Acknowledge
11. Patience
12. Tenderness
13. Jesus
14. Humility and Goodwill
15. Quiet/stillness
16. Treasure Friendships
17. Know
18. Shelter
19. Joy
20. Trust
21. Peace
22. Praise
23. Nearer
24. Gratitude
25. Rest
26. Gentleness
27. Peace
28. Tender
29. Angels
30. Wisdom.

End of month reflections for September 2005

Today is a new day. Begin with a grateful spirit. You are protected from the evil one. Give love by taking time during the day to rest in God's care. You are safe in his presence. God is love.

Be present to him. Acknowledge his presence, his love. Have patience and tenderness with yourself. Jesus loves you. Create within yourself a sense of humility and good will. It is in the quiet stillness of the spirit that you remember to treasure friendships. You experience the shelter of their love. There is great joy in the trust of friendships. They give peace to your soul. Praise God for his gift of friends.

With a heart full of gratitude, we know that God is nearer than any earthly friend. To learn of God's gentleness, rest in his presence. You will come away from union with God as a more loving friend to those who need your tenderness.

Angels are watching over you. Seek wisdom from scripture. Wisdom is knowledge guided by understanding.

Words for October 2005

1. Trust
2. Meek
3. Quietness
4. Love
5. Blessings
6. All is well
7. Rejoice
8. Sweetness
9. Love
10. Simple
11. Silence
12. Patience
13. Honor
14. Listen
15. Faith
16. Praise
17. Calm
18. Peace
19. Hope
20. Accept
21. Live
22. Spirit
23. Trust
24. Glorify
25. Humble
26. Friends
27. Comfort
28. Do right
29. Be still
30. Quiet
31. Seek righteousness.

End of month reflections for October 2005

Trust God! Have a meek quietness about yourself. Radiate God's love. Blessings will flow. Remember, "All is well." Rejoice always. Have a genuine sweetness about yourself. Love tenderly by keeping your life simple. Be silent before the Lord. Have patience with difficult people. They will come around when you show them respect and honor by listening to their heart. Have faith in where they are in their walk with God. Praise them for the work they do. Accept them and love them. Live, love, and laugh with them. Smile more. Let God's spirit lead you.

Trust God and give glory to his name. Be humble before the Lord. God will help you to love, honor, and cherish people. Do right by others and do right to yourself. Give people the comfort they need. Be still in God's presence. Quiet your soul before God. This will help you to be slow to anger. Seek righteousness.

"Be still . . . And know that I am God" (Ps. 46:11).

This is what is needed. The deep quiet of Psalm 46:11. In all our busyness of the day, take time to be still in the presence of God. This helps you to make good life decisions.

Words for November 2005

1. Joy
2. Give
3. Friendship
4. Jesus
5. Comfort
6. Praying
7. Kindred
8. Good
9. Friend
10. Simple
11. Trust
12. Prayer
13. Do good
14. Bright firm hope
15. Trust
16. Hope
17. Quiet
18. Patience
19. Smile
20. Grace
21. Love
22. Strength
23. Thanks
24. Grace
25. Listen
26. Peace
27. Spirit of the Living God
28. Guide me
29. Safety
30. Friendships

End of month reflections for November 2005

Beautiful, heartfelt joy comes with the gift of true friendships with Jesus at the core. There is great comfort when you have a praying kindred spirit. Good friends keep it simple. They trust each other with prayer request. They try to do good by each other, offering bright firm hope. They hope for the best. True friends can be quiet together. They have patience when you need it most. Their smile can brighten any gray day. They grace your life with their love. The strength of their caring is beyond measure. They are thankful for your friendship. God's grace and peace is certain to follow as you listen with your heart to each other.

Peace flows in our heart as the Spirit of the Living God guides us to the safety of his presence through the love in our friendships.

"A faithful friend is a sturdy shelter; he who finds one finds a treasure" (Sir. 6:14, NAB).

Words for December 2005

1. Responsibility
2. Vision
3. Love
4. Kindness
5. Encouragement
6. Give
7. Hope
8. Faith
9. Lead
10. Wait
11. Joy
12. Serve
13. Guidance
14. Light
15. Loving kindness
16. Faithfulness
17. Blessings
18. Hearts
19. Destiny
20. Cherish
21. Smile
22. All is well
23. Peace
24. Be still
25. Faith
26. Healthy
27. Good work
28. Friendship
29. Live life
30. Grace
31. Jesus.

LINDA F. STAFFORD

End of month reflections for December 2005

Our responsibility is to be responsible for the vision of love and kindness we give to others. Give large amounts of encouragement and hope to others. Lead them by your own faiths example. Wait for God to do his great work in their lives. He will because he loves them more than you can.

Joyfully serve the Lord. Seek his guidance. God will light the way with his loving kindness. Your faithfulness blesses hearts more than you will ever know. Your destiny is to love and to cherish. Remember to smile because all is well. To be at peace, be still and let your faith settle deeper inside your soul. Remain healthy in your thoughts and actions. Whatever your task may be, do good work. Develop great friendships as you live your life. God's grace is sufficient for all your needs. Jesus is always available for you. Trust God in all things.

2006

Words for January 2006

1. Reflection
2. Patient
3. Child of God
4. Change
5. Hope
6. Sunshine
7. Acceptance
8. Joy
9. Calm
10. Influence
11. Listen
12. Glad
13. Trust
14. Healing
15. Playfulness
16. Friends
17. Compassionate heart
18. Faithfulness
19. Home
20. Time
21. Thank you
22. Joy
23. Good
24. Faith
25. Safety
26. Generosity
27. Receive
28. Spirit
29. Resting
30. Conformation
31. Encouragement.

End of month reflections for January 2006

Reflection: What do you see when you look inside your soul? We all have the freedom to respond to God's grace. It is our own choice. Choose wisely. Trust in God.

"My grace is sufficient for you, for power is made perfect in weakness" (2 Cor. 12:8).

Be patient and kind to yourself. You are a child of God. If you see a need for change . . . change.

This change will keep hope every day for a sunshine-giving life. Acceptance of the joy in your soul brings a calming influence into your spiritual listening heart. Be glad that you have trust in the healing art of playfulness.

Enjoy your friends. Have a compassionate heart toward all. Be thankful for their faithfulness, and in turn, be faithful. Stay home when you can to enjoy the time to yourself. Rest and relax. Remember to say "thank you" with a spirit of joy and good will. Keep the faith. Safety is found in God's presence. Keep a spirit of generosity in your thoughts. You will receive what you think. To get the confirmation and encouragement you need for your life's journey, keep your spirit open to the resting time you need.

Words for February 2006

1. Gentle
2. Peace
3. Praise
4. Rest
5. Walk
6. Healing
7. Home
8. Trust
9. Silence
10. Positive
11. Light
12. Sight
13. Encouragement
14. Love
15. Inspire
16. Jesus
17. Grace
18. Encouragement
19. Grateful heart
20. Refreshing
21. Open
22. Trust
23. Spirit
24. Justified
25. Prayer
26. Understanding
27. Listen
28. Grace.

End of month reflections for February 2006

Let God's gentle love envelope your whole being. Let his peace fill your soul. Give God praise, every day in everything. Take time to rest in the loving presence of God. Walk very humbly with God. Let his healing love penetrate your hurting heart, mind, spirit, and soul.

Home is a good place to be. Appreciate your home. Take care of it. Trust in God's unfailing concern for your well-being. Sit in silence. Listen to the Holy Spirit. Remain positive even in troubled times. Count your blessings. In this way, you let God's light shine through you. Your sight is made clearer. Your views are better. Give people the encouragement and love that they so desperately need. Inspire people to do what is right. When you are afraid, say the name of Jesus. He will help. God's amazing grace will save you. Be a channel of encouragement to those who are feeling down.

Have a grateful heart and attitude. Spirit rest is refreshing to your soul. Be open to the God-given spirit rest. Follow the spirit of the living God. You will be justified. God will move people and things (heaven and earth) to help make things right again. He gave his son because he loves us so much. Don't forget to say your prayers. God is waiting. He is listening and longing to hear from you.

God understands. He loves and he cares. Listen in silence. Your soul will connect. You are loved through God's amazing grace. Sing praise to the great creator.

Words for March 2006

1. Accepting
2. Words
3. Pray
4. Holy
5. Comfort
6. Laugh
7. Peace
8. Joy
9. Kindly
10. Simplicity
11. Reflect
12. Goodness
13. Peace
14. Wait
15. Listen
16. Quiet
17. Positive
18. Now
19. Embrace
20. Acceptance
21. All is Well

22. Bloom
23. Guide
24. Respect
25. Perseverance
26. Generous
27. Press on
28. Obedience
29. Respect
30. Laughter
31. Expect.

End of month reflections for March 2006

Accepting the wise words of our elders and prayerfully pondering the holy meaning these have for our life will bring us comfort, peace, and the ability to laugh again. Look kindly on our elders. Their simplicity is a great art. Reflect on their unique goodness. Wait patiently for guidance. Listen closely to the Holy Spirit. Quiet yourself until the positive Holy Spirit flows. Now, you can respond to life by embracing and accepting the good. All is well.

Bloom and grow where God has placed you. Respect the leading of the Holy Spirit. Perseverance in a holy life is for everyone's good. Don't give up. Be generous with yourself. Keep pressing on, obeying the commandments. Respect yourself. Laughter is a very healthy activity. Expect miracles. God is in control.

Words for April 2006

1. Kiss
2. Blessings
3. Service
4. Peace of the Lord
5. Rest
6. Begin
7. Rise
8. Joyful
9. Grace
10. Silence
11. Discipline
12. Trust
13. Gentle
14. Good
15. Calm
16. Love
17. Rejoice
18. Grateful
19. Expect
20. Joy
21. Faith
22. Circle
23. Guidance
24. Spirit
25. Courage
26. Secure
27. Appreciation
28. Knowing
29. Harmony
30. Sunshine.

End of month reflections for April 2006

April is the kiss of spring. Blessings abound in the service of life's new growth. The peace of the Lord is found in rest for your soul as you begin to rise joyfully at the day set before you. God's grace is found in silence and in discipline. Trust in the gentle touch of goodness. Calm results from true love as you rejoice with a grateful heart.

Expect the miracle of joy to return as your faith circle gives you guidance from the spirit of courage. Rest secure in the appreciation of knowing God's harmony in nature. Live in the sunshine; we will understand it all in time.

Words for May 2006

1. Respect
2. Smile
3. Home
4. Share
5. Quiet
6. Awake
7. Grace
8. Faith
9. Prayer
10. Listen
11. Unity
12. Protection
13. Joy
14. Tender
15. Faith
16. Listen
17. Sacred
18. Light
19. Quiet
20. Guide
21. Obedience
22. Journey
23. Thankfulness
24. Much
25. Wisdom
26. Sincere
27. Ponder
28. Contentment
29. Wait
30. Praise
31. Open.

End of month reflections for May 2006

Have a deep respect for all of life. Smile more often. Love being at home. Learn to share yourself with yourself. Spend quality quiet time alone with your thoughts. Be awakened to the Holy Spirit dwelling in you. Accept the grace of others faith and their prayers. Live by listening attentively to the heart of others. Unity is the key to success.

God's protection supports your efforts. Keep joy in your life. Keep tender moments of faith close to your listening heart. Let the sacredness of life light your way. The Holy Spirit is a quiet guide. Obedience to the promptings of the Holy Spirit is vital on your life's journey. Thankfulness provides joy. Much wisdom is needed. Be very sincere in your thanksgiving. Ponder your response to difficult situations. Contentment is forthcoming. Just wait patiently. Praise and continue to be open to the Holy Spirit.

Words for June 2006

1. Come
2. Silence
3. Praise
4. Spirit
5. Life
6. Grow
7. Encouragement
8. Faith
9. Lead
10. Faithful
11. Peace
12. Move
13. Trust
14. Journey
15. Grow
16. Confidant
17. Jesus
18. Abba
19. Obedience
20. Encouragement
21. Moderation
22. Freedom
23. Peace
24. Quietly
25. Compassion
26. Secure
27. Hope
28. Love
29. Safe
30. Understanding heart.

End of month reflections for June 2006

Come, Holy Spirit, come into the silence that lifts hearts to praise. Allow the Spirit of life to grow. Give encouragement to each weary soul. Let faith be your constant companion. Lead faithfully, showing peace in your life. Move as the Holy Spirit prompts you. Trust God on your life journey. Glory waits. Be confident in Jesus's great love for you. God is our Abba. The father loves so deeply. Be obedient in Jesus. Obey his commands. When you need encouragement, turn to Abba.

Moderation is the best way to keep healthy. Freedom comes in surrender to God's will. Peace will flow. Life is good. Quietly go about your business giving God's compassion to those who are in need (including yourself). You are secure in God's loving arms. Hope on, love on, you are safe in the everlasting care of God. Keep an understanding heart for those who are hurting.

Words for July 2006

1. Cheer
2. Faith
3. Loving
4. Bless
5. Trust
6. Faithful heart
7. Courage
8. Listen
9. Joy
10. Remember
11. Speak
12. Calm
13. Faith
14. Grace
15. Secure
16. Relax
17. Restore
18. Time
19. Seeing
20. Thanksgiving
21. Practical
22. Seek
23. Blessings
24. Message
25. Trust
26. Acceptance
27. Help
28. Trust
29. Joy
30. Rest
31. Life.

End of month reflections for July 2006

Active listening and you shall hear the Holy Spirit speaking be of good cheer. A cheerful heart will increase your faith. Lovingly bless others. Trust in their basic goodness. Have a faithful heart full of courage as you listen with joy. Remember the wonderful goodness of the Lord. Speak in a calm manner. Have a great faith, letting God's amazing grace shower you with blessings. We are secure with God's love and protection.

Relax tired nerves to restore a positive outlook. Take time for yourself. Be open to seeing all the goodness in your life with heartfelt thanksgiving. Be practical in what you do. Seek the highest blessings, leaving a message of hope, trust, and acceptance to all. Be a help when needed. Trust yourself to do what is right in the spirit of joy for the rest of your life.

Words for August 2006

1. Contentment
2. Restore
3. Praise
4. Heart
5. Quiet
6. Apart
7. Light
8. Safe
9. Kindness
10. Cheerfulness
11. Care
12. Patience
13. Harmony
14. Life
15. Gentle
16. Perseverance
17. Thankful
18. Supportive
19. Listen
20. Angel
21. Work
22. Sunshine
23. Adoration
24. Holy Spirit
25. Love
26. Grace
27. Quietness
28. Faith
29. Believe
30. Give
31. Share.

End of month reflections for August 2006

What price contentment? What will restore peace? Give heartfelt praise to the Lord. Find a quiet place that is apart from distractions. A safe place that is full of light. Let the kindness of the Lord envelope you. You will come away with cheerfulness in your life. Be patient in seeking the harmony of a life well lived. Be gentle with yourself as with a small child.

Persevere in thankfulness. Be supportive as you listen to your family and your friends concerns. Be like an angel working to bring sunshine to others. Show adoration to God the Father, Jesus, the Son, and to the Holy Spirit. Keep love foremost in your thoughts. God's grace flows in the quietness of a faith filled soul. Keep believing in the blessings of giving and sharing love.

Words for September 2006

1. Love	11. Courage	21. Follow
2. Understand	12. Thanks	22. Joy
3. Receive	13. Peace	23. Near
4. Listen carefully	14. Faith	24. Wisdom
5. Surprise	15. Rest	25. Peace
6. Work	16. Peace	26. Listen
7. Respond	17. Know	27. Respect
8. Help	18. Shelter	28. Kindness
9. Faithful	19. Enjoy	29. Angels
10. Open	20. Trust	30. Knowledge.

End of month reflections for September 2006

When you receive and give the gift of love, you will be lifted to a new understanding of the meaning of a life well lived. Listen carefully, life is full of surprises. Faithfully work at your job, respond wholeheartedly to each task. Seek help when needed by respectfully opening the line of communication. Be courageous in giving thanks for the help you receive.

Be at peace with your faith community. Rest until the peace comes. Know that you are loved. Seek shelter from the storms of life. Enjoy your journey. Trust the events as these unfold. Follow the promptings of the Holy Spirit. Bring joy to others. Hold them near to your heart. Seek the wisdom that brings peace of mind. Listen to those you respect and trust. Show kindness as God's holy angels continue to minister to all. Seek knowledge in all areas of your life. Knowing brings understanding.

Words for October 2006

1. Seek
2. Guardian angels
3. Quietness
4. Calm
5. Courage
6. Peace of Soul
7. Openness
8. Joyful
9. Love
10. Simple
11. Father
12. Faithful
13. Trust
14. Hear
15. Plenty
16. Order
17. Positive
18. Faith
19. Angels
20. Simple
21. Tender
22. Seeking
23. Wellness
24. Centered
25. Goodness
26. Peace
27. Gentleness
28. Support
29. Faith
30. Gratitude
31. Words.

End of month reflections for October 2006

Seek the Lord where he may be found, in the silence of your soul, in the beauty of nature, in each other, in his Holy Sacred Scripture. Guardian angels are everywhere. Trust their guiding, guarding wings. (Go with the flow.) In quietness and in calm, seek the Lord. Take courage in doing God's will. Peace of soul, Christ peace is yours for the asking.

Be open to openness. Receive God's joyful love. Take the simple path of love. Your father in heaven is always faithful. Trust in all that you hear from the Holy Spirit. Plenty of help is available just ask. Order your lives in a positive way. Keep the faith. Angels are all around. It is a simple task to just believe. Tender touches will guide your seeking spirit.

Wellness is yours when you keep yourself centered in goodness, peace, and gentleness. Support one another in faith. Show your gratitude in loving words of wisdom. Be kind to one another.

Words for November 2006

1. Dignity
2. Give
3. Receive
4. Jesus
5. Love
6. Unity
7. Spirit
8. Strong
9. Positive
10. Faith
11. Wonder
12. Little
13. Discern
14. Courage
15. Thanks
16. Happy
17. Joy
18. Friendship
19. Hope
20. Love
21. Joy
22. Journey
23. Thanksgiving
24. Blessings
25. Work
26. Mystery
27. Protected
28. Believe
29. Care
30. Refuge.

End of month reflections for November 2006

Where is your dignity? It is found in your relationships. How good are your relationships? Your dignity is defined in your relationship with God. He gives examples of how to live your life. Read and study the Bible. You will receive nourishment from the "word made flesh" Jesus. God's love will bring unity of spirit and a strong positive faith.

Wonder of wonder, little by little, day by day, you will be able to discern God's will. Take courage; give thanks for the gifts of insight into the wonderful ways God is leading. Happy the person who brings joy, hope, and love to their friendships.

Find a way to add joy as you journey through your day. One day at a time. Focus on today, giving thanks as blessings are occurring. Your true work on earth is to be more loving. No mystery here. Just be more loving. You can rest, knowing you are protected by a loving God. Care enough to believe. When storms come, and storms will come, seek refuge in the loving embrace of God. You will be able to face tomorrow. Whatever tomorrow may bring, God is in control and all will be well.

Words for December 2006

1. Grace	12. Goodness	23. Wonder
2. Pray	13. Love	24. Nearness
3. Silence	14. Assurance	25. Gift
4. Trust	15. Forgiveness	26. Journey
5. Peace	16. Joyful	27. Kinder
6. Faith	17. Time	28. Tender
7. Heart	18. Faith	29. Delight
8. Bloom	19. Time	30. Soft
9. Joy	20. Openness	31. Peace.
10. Friendship	21. Smile	
11. Seek	22. Light	

End of month reflections for December 2006

God's grace is sufficient for all your needs. Pray for God's grace to fill your life. In the silence of your heart, you will learn to trust your instincts. Peace will flow from your faith.

Keep your heart pure so you can bloom like a beautiful flower. Enjoy your friendships. Seek to be joyful by being a forgiving person. Faith is a time tested friend. In time your openness to the Holy Spirit will make sense to the decisions made in the stillness and quietness of your soul. Smile and light the way to all the wonder around you. God's nearness is a great gift as you journey through your days on earth.

Be kinder by being tender in your dealings with people. Take delight in doing what is right. Have a soft approach to all. The peace of Christ will flow to you and to those whom you meet and greet.

2008

Words for January 2008

1. Light of God
2. Focus
3. Healing
4. Silence
5. Forgiveness
6. Shine
7. Presence
8. Gifts
9. Seeking
10. Live in the Spirit
11. Empowered
12. Good
13. Friends
14. Gratitude
15. Encourage
16. Walk
17. Receive
18. Faith
19. Love
20. Peace
21. Safely
22. Living Presence
23. Joy
24. All is well
25. Happiness
26. Bless
27. Health
28. Rest
29. Trust
30. Confirmation
31. Care.

End of month reflections for January 2008

Keep the light of God's presence in your heart. Focus on his great love. Let his healing love transform your mind. Wait in silence for the forgiveness of sins. When you are forgiven, rise, shine and live in the presence of God's love. You have been given a beautiful gift.

While seeking God, you found love. Live in the Spirit of the Lord. You will be empowered by the Lord's will to be good and holy.

Your friends will see God through the love and support you give them. The gratitude you have for their friendship will help them in their walk with God. Receive their faith with love.

Let peace surround your presence as God leads you safely home. Living in the presence of the Holy Spirit is a true joy, knowing all is well. Happiness is a state of mind. Surrender your heart to God. Graciously give your blessing. Health comes to us better when we are rested and forgiven. Trust in the confirmation of God's love and care.

Words for February 2008

1. God's love
2. Protection
3. Believe
4. Praise
5. Comfort
6. Joyful
7. Light
8. Walk with God
9. Openness to change
10. Breath
11. Wait
12. Be faithful
13. Listen carefully
14. Hopeful
15. Inspire
16. Be calm
17. Truth
18. Forgiven again
19. Open
20. Safety
21. Time
22. Keep trusting
23. Encourage
24. Rest
25. Wisdom
26. Do right
27. Give thanks
28. Spirit
29. Silence.

End of month reflections for February 2008

God's love is steadfast and strong. His protection is lovingly overwhelming. Believe in God's goodness and love. Praise him. Seek his comfort through the joyful light of his presence.

As you walk with God, you open yourself to the changes necessary to make you whole again. Simply breathe in the breath of life, his spirit. No matter what happens, faithfully wait in anticipation for the Holy Spirit to guide you.

Listen carefully to the hopefulness of Spirit. Let the inspiration of the Holy Spirit dwell in the calmness of God's truth. His great love for you is true. Be open to your need of forgiveness again and again. There is safety in forgiving others and finding the time needed for healing. Trust in God's love and mercy. Being an encourager happens better after you are well rested. Wisdom flows from rest, helping you to do what is right. Give thanks to God for his love. Rest in his spirit; seek the silence of your soul to find contentment for your well-being. Be loving and kind to yourself.

Words for March 2008

1. Mercy
2. God's peace
3. God's presence
4. Care
5. Hear the good
6. Laughter of God
7. Joy
8. Friend
9. Spirit
10. Love
11. Praise the Lord
12. God is with us
13. Listen for God's voice
14. Only believe
15. Great faith
16. Wisdom
17. Light
18. Faithful
19. Courage
20. Prayer
21. Hope
22. Strength
23. Humble
24. Joyful
25. Kindness
26. Guide
27. Light
28. Joy of the Lord
29. God's love
30. Divine mercy
31. Put it in God's hands.

End of month reflections for March 2008

Lord, have mercy on us and grant us your peace. Realizing God's presence lets us know how much he cares. Listen and hear the good in others. Listen for the laughter of God in the joyful smiles of a friend. A forever friend lifts our spirits and adds beautiful love to our life.

Praise the Lord for his many blessings. God is with us (Emmanuel.) Listen for God's voice. Only believe, all things are possible with God. Have a great faith by seeking wisdom. Let the light of God's love open the eyes of our heart to the wonder of who he is to us.

Remain faithful. Be stout hearted waiting for the Lord with courage. Be a person of prayer. Our hope is in the Lord. He is our strength. Keep a humble, merry heart. Choose to be joyful, showing kindness. Let Christ light guide our speech. Live our life in the joy of the Lord. Show God's love to others. God's Divine Mercy has given us a new life. We put our lives in God's hands and we live our lives trusting in his care.

Words for April 2008

1. Open
2. Live in the light of God's Presence
3. Simple
4. Love
5. Faith
6. Humble
7. Gifts
8. Acceptance
9. Shine
10. Pray
11. Focus
12. Trust
13. Laugh
14. Keep seeking
15. Home
16. Forgive
17. Quiet time
18. Happy heart
19. Presence
20. Closeness of God
21. Peacefulness
22. Peace
23. Blessings
24. Remain in God's love
25. Soften heart
26. Faithful
27. Joy
28. Joy of the heart
29. Openness
30. Protection
31. Spirit.

End of month reflections for April 2008

Open your heart to the love around you. Live in the light of God's presence. Keep your life as simple as possible. Show love for the faith you have received. Be humble in accepting the gifts of acceptance by others. Their acceptance helps you to shine. Pray for yourself. Pray for others.

Keep your focus on the presence of the living God. Trust in the laughter of your heart. Keep seeking the Lord's will. Take time to rest at home. This rest will lead to a happy, loving heart. Practice living in the presence of God. As you let peacefulness envelop you, peace will flow from your heart. You will be a blessing to others. By remaining in God's loving presence, your heart will be softened, your faithfulness will grow stronger, and you will receive the gift of true joy. The joy of a thankful heart will be yours as you remain open to the protection and guidance of the Holy Spirit.

Words for May 2008

1. The Lord's presence
2. Spend quiet time with the Lord
3. Know God/ know love
4. Simple
5. Choose a good life
6. Be open to the truth
7. Love
8. Peace maker
9. Laughing God
10. Little is much
11. Spirit
12. Knowing
13. Persevere
14. Deeply loved
15. Humble
16. Caring for others
17. Keep the peace
18. Kindness
19. Present moment
20. God's gracious gifts
21. Sing praise
22. Yes Lord
23. Praise
24. Refuge
25. The greater Gift
26. Strength
27. Receive
28. More love
29. Be humble
30. Praise the Lord
31. Blessings.

End of month reflections for May 2008

By spending quiet time with the Lord, you learn to live your life in the presence of God. You come to know God's great love. Simply choose to live a good life, being open to his love and his truths. Be a peace keeper even when that means disturbing the peace.

Enjoy a loving, laughing God. Lighten up! Realize that little is much when God is in it. His living, loving Spirit changes everything. Knowing God's love helps you to persevere. Just knowing you are loved deeply and fully by God keeps you humble in your need to care for others. Strive to keep the peace by showing kindness. Focus on the present moment, the now of life. Be thankful for God's many gracious gifts. Like the birds in the early morning, sing praise. Listen! Say yes to the Lord's leading. Praise the Lord always. When things start to disturb you, seek a safe place, a refuge to rest in God's loving hands (the best safe place to be is with God.) The greatest gift is always showing love. Gain strength through love. Be humble, yet joyful in your love. Praise the Lord for his many blessings!

> *"Take these words of mine into your heart and soul. Bind them at your wrist as a sign, and let them be a pendent on your forehead . . ."* (Deut. 11:18).

Words for June 2008

1. God's word
2. Receive
3. Kindness
4. Courage
5. Be thankful
6. Friendships
7. Beautiful
8. Jesus
9. God's peace
10. Trust
11. Right choice
12. Goodness
13. Honesty
14. Today
15. Bounty
16. Be at peace
17. Jesus
18. Hopeful
19. Faith
20. Speak truth
21. Charity
22. Grace
23. Rest
24. Light
25. Friendship
26. Guide
27. Simple
28. Enjoy the Lord
29. Encouragement
30. Follow the Lord.

End of month reflections for June 2008

The Bible is God's word, divinely inspired. Read the Bible to receive God's instructions and love. The Bible teaches kindness, forgiveness, love and the courage we need to face life. God is our goal, live every day for him. Be thankful to be alive knowing that little is much as long as you keep seeking.

Cherish the gifts of beautiful friendships. Jesus is your best forever friend. God's peace comes through trust and making the right choices. His goodness is your saving grace. Honesty is the best choice. To be at peace and to have a hopeful life giving faith, speak the truth. Have a spirit of charity when dealing with others reputation. God's grace has been given to you. Take the time to rest in God's love and care. Let his light into your life so that you can be light for others. God's friendship is always available. Be open to receive. Seek his guidance. Listen to the Holy Spirit. Keep your life simple. Enjoy the Lord every day. Be a source of encouragement to others by following the Lord Jesus Christ all the days of your life. Live well by loving.

Words for July 2008

1. Emmanuel
2. Courage
3. Beautiful
4. Listen to Holy Spirit
5. Truthful
6. Light
7. Praise God
8. Thankful
9. Joyful
10. Give
11. Respect
12. Peace
13. Speak words of encouragement
14. Hope
15. Secret
16. Hear what others say
17. Be still and at peace
18. Freeing
19. Love
20. Understanding heart
21. Praise the Lord
22. Shine
23. Calm
24. Understand other's point
25. Wonderful
26. God's presence
27. Treasure
28. Faith
29. Listen
30. Words
31. Purpose.

LINDA F. STAFFORD

End of month reflections for July 2008

    Because God lives among us (Emmanuel) we take courage in his presence. With a beautiful smile, we listen to the Holy Spirit's message of truth. Let your light shine as you praise God in the stillness of your soul. Be thankful for the help that comes your way. Be joyful in giving respect to those who request your help. Be at peace with yourself. Speak words of encouragement and hope. Keep the secrets entrusted to you. Hear what others are saying. Be still, at peace, freeing your heart to love and understand.

    Keep praising the Lord by rising every day and letting your light shine in calmness. Try to understand others point of view. Life is really wonderful in God's loving presence. Treasure your quiet times with God. Your faith will grow stronger as you listen to the words of the Bible. Be open to your purpose. Your purpose is to love.

Words for August 2008

1. Bountiful
2. Harvest
3. Bless
4. Courage
5. Kindness
6. Joy in the journey
7. Heart of God
8. Faith
9. Hope
10. Charity
11. Peace
12. Guide
13. Caring
14. Forgive
15. Trust
16. Holy Spirit
17. Beautiful
18. Keep on keeping on
19. Divine love
20. Trustworthy
21. Grace
22. Sunlight
23. Obedience
24. Possible
25. Peace of the Lord
26. Integrity
27. Quiet confidence
28. Beauty
29. Jesus
30. Give
31. God's love.

End of month reflections for August 2008

God's bountiful harvest blesses us in all our needs. Courage and kindness give joy for the journey as you seed your heart with God's love. Live with faith, hope, and charity to be at peace as God guides you to have a caring, forgiving heart.

Trust the inspiration of the Holy Spirit. Live a beautiful life in troubled times as you keep on keeping on. Know that Divine love is trustworthy. Grace and sunlight will come as you follow the path of obedience to God's loving protection. All things are possible with the Lord, our master, savior, and friend. The peace of the Lord and quiet confidence will be yours as you walk in the integrity of God's amazing love.

Words for September 2008

1. God
2. Loving heart
3. Supportive
4. Sing
5. Trust
6. Encourage
7. Church family
8. The Blessed Virgin Mary
9. Faithful
10. Believe
11. Love
12. Light
13. Together
14. Forgiveness
15. Silence
16. Quietness
17. Happy Spirit
18. Little is much
19. Joy
20. Seeing
21. God loves
22. Sing praise
23. Do right
24. Secure
25. Respect
26. Service
27. Happy heart
28. Enjoy
29. Generous
30. Truth.

End of month reflections for September 2008

God is the great I AM, who has an awesome loving heart. Learn from him. Be supportive, caring, and loving. Be a living, singing, joyful presence. Trust in God's love and care. Be an encourager. Along with your church family, all the angels and saints, and the Blessed Virgin Mary (the mother of God) be very thankful and be faithful to God. Be a believer in love, lighting the way for each other.

Learn to forgive, to be silent about the shortcomings of others. In calm, quietness you can regain a happy spirit. You don't need to overdo things. Little is much when God is in control. Give joy away. See and believe in God's loving presence. Sing joyful praise. Always do what is right. Be secure in God's love. Love, respect, and serve others with a smile and a happy heart. Enjoy today by being generous in the wisdom of the truth.

Words for October 2008

1. A prayer
2. Guardian angels
3. Quiet reserve
4. Make a difference
5. Safe
6. Mercy
7. All is well
8. Be brave
9. Heartfelt love
10. Keep it simple
11. Praise the Lord
12. Angels
13. Be faithful
14. Truly love
15. Holy Spirit
16. Bless others
17. Faithful
18. Goodness
19. Be truthful
20. Be a blessing
21. Christ peace
22. Harmony
23. Trust
24. Listen
25. God's grace
26. Compassion
27. Be kind
28. Seek God
29. All is well
30. Patience
31. Value.

End of month reflections for October 2008

Say a prayer every day in praise and thanksgiving for the wonderful love of God. Call on the protection of the guardian angels. Go through your day with a quiet reserve, knowing that a peaceful disposition makes a difference. You are safe in the loving mercy of God's protection.

Even in difficult circumstances, you can be assured that God is in control and all is well. Be brave with others, showing heartfelt love. Be a person of peace, by keeping your life simple. Give praise to the Lord with the angels. Be a faithful witness. Truly love your family and friends. Trust in the promptings of the Holy Spirit. Be a blessing to others by blessing them with kindness. Be faithful and true to the goodness in yourself. Be a blessing of Christ peace by bringing harmony and trust as you listen with God's grace guiding you. Show compassion by being very kind when you speak. When things are troublesome, seek God first. As you remember that all is well, have patience and value your quiet time with the Lord.

Words for November 2008

1. Joy
2. In the palm of God's hand
3. Give
4. Jesus
5. Joyful
6. Listen
7. Honesty
8. Abundance
9. Blessings
10. Faith
11. Appreciate
12. God's Goodness
13. Peace
14. God's peace
15. Quietness of heart
16. Trust
17. Love God
18. Guidance
19. Praise the Lord
20. Be open
21. Jesus
22. God's strength
23. Healing
24. Give
25. Humble
26. Beauty
27. Share
28. Believe
29. Friendship
30. Be careful.

End of month reflections for November 2008

Joy is abundant. You are in the palm of God's loving hands. Learn to give even in the lean times. Jesus is always there for you. Be joyful in the hope that he cares and listens. Honesty in your relationship with God will bring many blessings.

Keep the faith by being consistent in what really matters. God's goodness will bring you peace. Quiet your heart and trust in the love that is God. Seek his guidance. Praise the Lord and be open to his presence.

When strife comes, say the name of Jesus. God's strength will sustain you and bring a healing calm. Give kindness to others. Be humble letting the beauty of God's love be shared in your actions, your belief, and your trust in his unfailing love.

Be forever thankful for friendships. Be careful not to take friends for granted. Friendships are vital. Be careful not to jeopardize friendships.

Words for December 2008

1. Walk humbly with God
2. Stay near to God
3. Healing
4. Listen
5. Hope
6. The Love of God
7. Quietly present
8. Clear headed
9. Simply quiet yourself
10. Rest
11. Kind hearted
12. Trust in God
13. Open Heart
14. Listen
15. Guide
16. Wait
17. Acceptance with love
18. Know God
19. Be not afraid
20. Jesus
21. Give thanks
22. Quiet your heart
23. God's love
24. Humble
25. Love
26. Helpful
27. Safely home
28. Friendship
29. Love
30. Peace
31. Do right.

End of month reflections for December 2008

As the day unfolds, walk humbly with your God. Stay very near to God throughout the day. Let his healing love cure your hurts. Listen to his wisdom as you place your hope in the love of God. Be quietly present and remain clear headed when dealing with others.

Remember to simply quiet yourself by resting in God's loving presence. Be kind hearted to all who come your way. Trust in God's care and guidance. Keep an open heart by truly listening to God. Wait for promptings of the Holy Spirit. Accept others with God's love in mind. You can only do this if you know God's love for yourself. Do not be afraid of the journey. God is with you. God is, Jesus is, the Holy Spirit is. Give thanks for this truth.

In the busyness of each day, take time to quiet your heart and mind. Reflect on God's love. Be humble before the Lord. Love him with all your heart.

Be a helpful person. At the end of the day, return safely home to bask in the warmth of God's tender care. Be faithful in all your friendships. Love deeply. Be at peace by always doing what is right and good.

2009

Words for January 2009

1. Encourage
2. Faith
3. Wait
4. God's light
5. Little is much
6. Peace of God
7. Listen
8. Love
9. Stay calm
10. Be kind
11. Be positive
12. Be helpful
13. Be humble
14. Sit with a friend
15. Relax
16. Be happy
17. All is well
18. Faith
19. Heart
20. Wait
21. Harmony
22. Thank you
23. Joyful spirit
24. Goodness
25. Guidance
26. Pass on the faith
27. Kindness
28. Guide
29. Encouragement
30. Joyful peace
31. Hope.

End of month reflections January 2009

I am encouraged by the faith of my friends as they wait in the light of God's love. They realize that little is much when they let God have control. They receive peace from God as they listen with love. They learn from him to stay calm; to be kind, positive, helpful, and humble as they sit with others. Their friends can relax, be happy, and come to know that all is well. They share their faith from their heart as they wait in harmony with God's will for the answer to their prayers. They remember to say thank-you to God for his love.

Their joyful spirit and goodness gives guidance to my soul. Friends pass on the faith by the way they live. They guide with kindness and encouragement. The joyful peace they show gives hope to my spirit. Friends are much loved.

Words for February 2009

1. Treasures
2. Wisdom
3. Keep it simple
4. Trust
5. Grace
6. Angels
7. Quiet
8. Joyful
9. God's healing touch
10. Trust
11. Tender
12. Love
13. Endurance
14. Faith
15. Rest
16. Hope
17. Do right
18. Healing touch
19. Jesus
20. Listen carefully
21. Great faith
22. Comforts of home
23. Prayer
24. Praise the Lord
25. Quiet time
26. Spiritual
27. Freeing
28. Kindness.

End of month reflections for February 2009

Treasure the wisdom in keeping life simple. Trust in the grace you receive by the presence of the angels. Quiet your spirit and joyfully receive God's healing touch. Trust in his tender love and care.

Endurance strengthens your faith but always find time to rest. Put your hope in the Lord. Always, I say it again, always do what is right. Receive the healing touch from Jesus, the Son of the Living God. To gain a great faith, listen carefully to God's word. Cherish the comforts of home as you rest in prayer. Lift your praise to the Lord, who made heaven and earth.

Spend quiet spiritual time in the Lord's presence to receive a freeing of what troubles you. "Never trouble—trouble until trouble—troubles you." Remember the kindness of the Lord and, in turn, be kind. Light a candle today. Love one another.

Words for March 2009

1. Spiritual journey
2. Balance
3. Care deeply
4. Listen to God's whisper
5. Thy will be done
6. Waiting before God
7. Forgiveness
8. God's love
9. Sunshine
10. Love and laugh
11. Happiness
12. Joyful
13. One kind word
14. Lead me
15. Listen carefully
16. Be good
17. Rely on God
18. Be joyful
19. Lighten up
20. Compassion
21. God's grace
22. Joy smile
23. Quiet time at home
24. Angel
25. Be kind
26. Soul mate
27. All is well
28. Restful quiet love
29. Soul mate/ yes Lord
30. Heart full of love
31. Love.

End of month reflections for March 2009

We are on a spiritual journey. We must learn balance and care deeply about ourselves. Learn to listen to God's whispers. Honestly proclaim, "Thy will be done, Lord." To listen to God's whispers we must wait before God, resting in his loving presence. By humbly accepting the Lord's forgiveness and his great love, we can move into his sunshine. With our joyful smile, we can spread love and laughter. Take advantage of quiet time at home. Let God's angels guide and protect your coming and your going. Thank you, Lord, for your angels.

We create happiness and many joyful memories by being kind. One kind word is so much to a soul mate from a soul mate. Lord, lead us and guide us, help us to know that all will be well. In the restful quiet of God's love, we learn to listen carefully to each other. Say your "yes" to the Lord. Rely on God. It is God who gives us a heart so full of love. Show compassion. Live well.

Words for April 2009

1. Guide to grace
2. Do right
3. Mary
4. Mother of God
5. Divine Mercy
6. Strength
7. Home
8. Light
9. Joyful
10. Strength
11. Friend
12. Faithful
13. Forgive
14. Gold
15. Understanding
16. There is hope
17. Be gentle
18. Keep calm
19. Listen
20. Gift
21. The peace of the Lord
22. Treasure
23. Simple
24. God is in control
25. Caring heart
26. Beautiful
27. Simple
28. Kind words
29. Trusting in God
30. Blessings
31. Listen.

End of month reflections for April 2009

Guide me, Lord, give me your grace. Help me to do what is right. Mary, Mother of God, pray for me. Lord, I need your Divine Mercy to give me the strength needed for the challenges of life.

Take time to enjoy your home. Treasure and take care of your home, your body, your friendships, and your life. Live in the light of God's love. Keep your life simple so you can live joyfully. Know that God is in control. Gaining strength from restfulness, you develop a caring heart.

Friendships become even more beautiful through faithfulness. Be a forgiving soul. Speak kind words of love. More pure than the purest gold is a loving friend. Trust in God for all to be well. Blessings are abundant. There is always hope. Listen carefully with your heart.

Be very gentle. Keep a calm spirit about yourself as you listen to others. Give people the gift of a listening heart. God is good—good all the time. Praise the Lord. Enjoy the Lord. Enjoy your friends. Keep them close.

Words for May 2009

1. Respect
2. Soul smile
3. Be at peace
4. Open hearts
5. God within
6. Walk in the Light of God's love
7. Goodness
8. Have faith
9. We matter
10. Be calm
11. Cherish
12. Joy
13. Do right
14. Love
15. Spiritual
16. Love and Laughter
17. Blessings
18. Prayer
19. Do the right thing
20. Live in the light of God's love
21. Trust
22. True friendship
23. Listen carefully
24. Treasure
25. Love one another
26. Hold to God's hand
27. Work
28. Giver
29. Blessings
30. Hope
31. Unity.

End of month reflections for May 2009

Respect each other's place of prayer and worship. Your soul smile comes from doing the right things. Be at peace by living in the light of God's love. Open your heart to trust God's presence in true friendships. Walk in the light of God's love. Let the goodness that flows from this walk show as you listen carefully to the heart cries of others. Have faith in friendships. Treasure your times together. Know that "we" matter. Love one another by being calm and devoted. Hold to God's hand.

Cherish the work you are called to do. Be thankful with a joyful heart. Do the right thing by being a giver of many blessings. There is hope for the future. Develop a spiritual unity and a keen awareness in all that is going on around you. Share lots of laughter.

Words for June 2009

1. Rest in God's presence
2. Surrender your heart to God
3. God's plan is for our good
4. Patience
5. God's touch
6. Generous
7. Friend
8. Be an encourager
9. Love
10. Do right
11. Pray
12. Treasure
13. Trust
14. Lead me
15. Silence
16. Calm
17. Generous
18. Do good
19. Love
20. Quiet time at home
21. Be still
22. Be not afraid
23. Listen to God
24. Guardian angel
25. Keep on keeping on
26. Keep it simple
27. Laughter of God
28. Peace
29. Keep the faith
30. Count your blessings.

End of month reflections for June 2009

As you rest in God's loving presence, surrender your heart to him. You will come to realize that his plan is always for your good. Be patient with your life's work for today. Keep doing good deeds by allowing God's touch of love to overflow in your generous heart. Spend quiet time at home. Be open to friendships. Be a friend by being still and listening so you can be an encourager. Do not be afraid of love. Listen to God and do right. Be at rest in the care of your guardian angel. Pray for the strength you need to keep on keeping on during troubled times.

Treasure a simple life by trusting God. Enjoy the laughter of God. Let his love and joy lead you and give you peace. Many times in the silence of your heart, you can keep the faith, keep calm, and count your blessings.

Words for July 2009

1. God's goodness
2. All is well
3. Rested
4. Keep it simple
5. Be present
6. Grace
7. A prayerful heart
8. Thanksgiving
9. Healing
10. Love
11. Friend
12. Quiet time
13. Forgive
14. Be not afraid
15. Saving
16. Listen
17. Mercy
18. Trust
19. Joyful heart
20. Caring friends
21. Praise the Lord
22. Shine
23. Breathe
24. Live in God's presence
25. Be helpful
26. Enjoy the Lord
27. Joyful
28. Compassion
29. Breathe deeply
30. Accept
31. Patience.

End of month reflections for July 2009

God, in his goodness, gives us his life saving, joyfulness. He allows us to know that all is well. One of the simplest things we can do for others is to listen to their hearts and offer our deep compassion. To do this, we must be well rested. Also, we know personally and appreciate the mercy that has been given to us.

When we are stressed out, we can breathe deeply; keep our lives simple, trust in the goodness of the Lord. Be present to others showing a joyful heart, patience and grace. Accept the love of caring friends and family because they truly are a gift and a blessing.

With a prayerful heart, praise God with thanksgiving. Let his sun shine in and through you to generate healing. These give you a fresh breath of life. Smile more, love more, and live more in the presence of God. Let God, shine through your speech and your actions. To be a more helpful compassionate friend, spend quiet time enjoying the peace of the Lord's presence. Learn the art of forgiveness and the ability to move past the hurts of life. Accept what you cannot change.

Words for August 2009

1. Love the Lord
2. Prayer time
3. Lighten up
4. Mercy
5. Faith
6. Spiritual
7. Miracles
8. Heart of Jesus
9. At home
10. Be generous
11. Follow the Lord's guiding hand
12. Share
13. God's presence
14. God's love
15. Mary
16. Mother of God
17. Peace of the Lord
18. Sunshine
19. Victory in Jesus
20. Free
21. Love will lift us up
22. Love
23. Insight
24. Seeing
25. Goodness
26. Gentleness
27. Busy
28. Love
29. Truth
30. Awareness
31. Hope.

End of month reflections for August 2009

Love the Lord and live in his sunshine. Spend quiet quality prayer time in his presence. There is victory in Jesus's name. Start to lighten up and be free to be who God wants you to be. Live your life in the Spirit of faith, hope, and love. Seek spiritual insight in the miracles of each day. The heart of Jesus is pure goodness. Be at home with God. Seek his gentleness so you can also be gentle, generous and kind to others. Follow the Lord's guiding hand. Share your insights with other busy souls.

God's presence is love. God's love is truth. As you ask others to pray for you, remember all the saints that have gone before us. Ask for their prayers, especially his mother, Mary. Seek a closer walk and awareness of God's will in your life by looking at the life these people lived. Let the peace of the Lord be your comfort as you hope for the sunshine of tomorrow. Love the Lord.

Words for September 2009

1. Live in God's light
2. Praise the Lord
3. God's presence
4. Thank you Lord
5. Our hope is in the Lord
6. Kindness and respect
7. Everlasting arms of God
8. Walk in Love
9. Lift up your hearts
10. Lord of mercy and compassion
11. See the good
12. I need you
13. Be good to yourself
14. Jesus
15. Goodness
16. Integrity
17. Mercy
18. Shelter
19. A thankful heart
20. Be wise
21. Yes Lord
22. Be joyful
23. Powerful
24. Slow down
25. Be calm
26. Live in the light
27. The church
28. Goodness
29. Angels of God
30. Acceptance.

End of month reflections for September 2009

Start living in the light of God's love by having a thankful heart, giving praise to the Lord. Seek wisdom. Be open to the Lord's leading. Seek God's presence in the events of the day. Say yes to the Lord from the promptings of the Holy Spirit. Watch for the presence and guiding of the angels. Even when you mess up, say thank you Lord for showing me that I messed up. Forgive yourself and move on with joy in your heart. Our hope is in the Lord.

Show others kindness and respect. Learn the art of slowing down your pace and resting in the everlasting arms of God. Walk in his love. Lift up your heart and thoughts living in the light of his mercy and compassion. See the good of the church. Go to church to honor God. We all need the Lord and we all need each other. Goodness is in us. Let the goodness grow. Be good to yourself. Angels of God have their mission; trust their leading. Jesus loves you. Accept his love. Live with integrity. Show God's mercy to others. Live in the shelter of God's love.

Words for October 2009

1. Heart of Jesus
2. Angels
3. Seek the Lord
4. Trust
5. Jesus
6. All is Well
7. Praise the Lord
8. Holy Spirit
9. Peace
10. Hearing the word of the Lord
11. Treasure
12. Compassion
13. Kindness
14. Goodness
15. Abundance
16. Acceptance
17. Faith
18. Balance
19. Sharing
20. Prepare
21. Listen
22. Quiet place
23. Humble
24. Praise God
25. Guidance
26. Blessings
27. Be kind
28. Be thoughtful
29. Treasure friendships
30. Joyful
31. Humble.

End of month reflections for October 2009

Sacred Heart of Jesus, help me as I try to balance my life. Thank you for sending your angels to protect and guard. Help me in my sharing with others. As I prepare to write today, I feel lost. The thoughts aren't flowing. I trust you, Lord. I am listening. Jesus, this is our time; our quiet place, come be with me.

I know that all is well. I humble myself before you, praise you and ask for the Holy Spirit's guidance. I let the peace and blessings flow through me. I hear your words. I treasure them in my heart. I need your help to be kind to the unkind, to show compassion to the hurting; to be thoughtful and considerate. Help me to especially show kindness to my friends and to treasure friendships. Let your goodness shine through.

I humble my heart before you. Lord, forgive me of my sins. I accept your forgiveness. I accept your love as I continue to walk on in faith, hope, and love.

"Make me understand the way of your precepts, and I will mediate on your wondrous deeds" (Ps. 119:27).

Words for November 2009

1. Blessed
2. Peace
3. Safe and Secure
4. Love
5. God's presence
6. Strength and grace
7. Trust
8. Give
9. Hold dear
10. Courage
11. Seek the wisdom of God
12. Considerate
13. Silence
14. Seek the Lord
15. Kind words
16. United
17. Courage
18. God's presence
19. Praise
20. Faith
21. Remember good
22. Love
23. Thank you
24. Angels
25. Care
26. Trust
27. Near to God
28. Seek the Lord
29. Do right
30. Journey.

End of month reflections for November 2009

Blessed is the one with enough courage to take a stand for peace. Live in God's presence. Be safe and secure in his loving embrace. Sing praise to the giver of love. Keep the faith by staying in God's presence. Acknowledge the good in others. Find strength and grace in their love. Trust their love. Say thank you when others give you help. Be aware of the holy angels and hold dear the care they give. Take courage, trusting in the wisdom you get from seeking God's council.

Be considerate of others by drawing nearer to God in the silence of your heart; seek the Lord. Do what is right. Stop the nonsense. Start using kind words as you journey through life. Stay united in friendship and united in love.

Words for December 2009

1. Mercy
2. Do right
3. Sunshine
4. Listen
5. Comfort
6. Repent
7. Deliverance
8. Trust

KNOWING GOD IS KNOWING LOVE

9. Blessings of Friends
10. Armor of the Lord
11. Light
12. Angels
13. Be positive
14. Trust
15. Generous
16. Grace
17. Bless
18. Holy Spirit
19. Jesus
20. Joyful
21. Courage
22. Open Door to heart
23. Bless us
24. Mercy
25. Jesus
26. God's plan
27. Discipline
28. Duty
29. Love
30. Patience
31. Simple.

End of month reflections for December 2009

Lord of mercy and compassion, have pity on me, a sinner. Send your Holy Spirit into my life. Help me to do right. Jesus, son of the living God, you are the sunshine of my life. Help me to live a joyful life as I listen with courage to your guiding words. Help me to bring comfort to the hurting hearts that I encounter on a daily basis. Open the door of my heart to repentance of my sins so that I may receive your blessings and deliverance. May your mercy prompt me to loving action and complete trust in your will for my life.

Jesus, I thank you for your mother. Mary, please pray for me. Jesus, I thank you for the blessings of friends that are part of God's plan. Often time, they are the armor of the Lord for me with their prayerful, loving support. The word of God is a powerful tool against despair. It is God's light that directs my path and teaches discipline. Thank you for your holy angels with duty to protect. They are a positive, guiding presence. Help me to show patience in the midst of strife. Help me to be generous, to live a simple, grace filled, blessed life.

2010

Words for January 2010

1. Pray for peace
2. Keep the Faith
3. Respect
4. Christ our light
5. Learn your lessons well
6. Relax
7. Wait
8. Peace
9. Goodness
10. Little
11. Take it to the Lord in prayer
12. Praise the Lord
13. Quiet moment
14. Walk with God
15. Friend
16. Love one another
17. Open heart
18. Obey the Lord
19. Healthy
20. Love
21. Kindness
22. Thank you Lord
23. Mary, Mother of God
24. Joy
25. Courage
26. Listen
27. Gift from God
28. At home alone
29. Sit quietly
30. Love lifts you up
31. Help me.

End of month reflections for January 2010

    Pray for peace. Obey the word of the Lord. Keep your faith strong and healthy by nourishing it with respect and love for others. Let Christ be your guiding light in showing kindness. Learn your lessons well from the mistakes you make. Relax and say thank you, Lord as you wait in his presence. Ask Mary, the Mother of God and all the saints to pray for you that you may obtain peace and joy through the goodness of the Lord.

Take courage and know that all is well. Do what you can when you realize that little is much as long as God is the inspiration. Listen to your heart. Take everything to God in prayer. Sing praise to the Lord. Accept his presence as gift. Seek quiet moments at home alone so that your walk with God will be fruitful. It is good to sit quietly and do nothing with a friend. Love will lift you higher than you can go alone. Love one another. Keep your life simple. Keep an open heart and help each other.

Words for February 2010

1. Eternal love
2. Protection
3. Believe
4. Rest
5. Praise the Lord
6. Wisdom
7. Light
8. Lead me
9. Stillness
10. Knowing
11. Keep doing right
12. Keep the Faith
13. Encouragement
14. Love
15. Kindness
16. Be calm
17. Truth
18. Blessing
19. Be good
20. Feast
21. Listen
22. Hope
23. Joyful
24. Blessings
25. Amazing
26. Do right
27. Goodness
28. Look up.

End of month reflections for February 2010

Take courage from the eternal love and protection of God. Keep believing in the goodness surrounding your life. Rest assured that you are loved. Praise the Lord for the wisdom and light that leads you to the stillness that brings calm. Knowing that all is well, keep doing what is right. Keep the faith. Be a source of encouragement and love by showing kindness to all. Keep a calm spirit about yourself. Know and accept the truth of all situations. Be a blessing. Accept blessings and do good works.

Feast on wisdom by reading and listening to God's word. Hope in the Lord with a joyful heart. Give your amazing, wonderful blessings with generosity. Many blessings will come back to you as you continue to do right. Surly the goodness and mercy of the Lord will follow you. Keep looking up to the source of all life. Receive God's blessings.

Words for March 2010

1. Gift
2. Truth
3. Be good
4. Patience
5. Lasting love
6. Freedom
7. Sunshine
8. Be a joyful person
9. Kind words
10. God's love
11. Don't be afraid
12. Caring
13. Compassion
14. Share in another's joy
15. Commitment
16. Holy angels
17. Open my eyes
18. Holy
19. Shielded
20. Walk in God's presence
21. God's faithfulness
22. Be not afraid
23. God is in control
24. God is faithful
25. God loves me
26. Be good and kind
27. Joy
28. Faith
29. Courage
30. Be calm
31. Depend on God.

End of month reflections for March 2010

Today is a gift. Open my eyes Lord to what is true. Truth is that God is in control and all is well. My responsibility is to be good, holy, to have patience with others and with myself. I am shielded by the Holy Spirit and God's everlasting love. As I walk in the presence of the living God, I realize the freedom available because of God's faithfulness. The sunshine of life is to be not afraid, to be a joyful person.

Speak kind words. Let go and let God be God. He is in control. God's love is faithful. God loves you so much. Be a caring, good, kind, compassionate person. Share in the joys of others. Respect their faith commitment and courage. The Holy Angels are watching over you. Be calm as you depend on God.

Words for April 2010

1. Tenderness
2. Goodness
3. Seek the Lord
4. Rejoice
5. Listen with your heart
6. Be at peace
7. Simplify
8. Living faithfully
9. Gentle encouragement
10. Good news
11. Good friend
12. Guide me
13. Trust
14. Faith
15. Love
16. God will make a way
17. Joyful
18. Love
19. Father God
20. Forgiveness
21. Blessings
22. Joy
23. Dear friend
24. Loving God
25. Spirit
26. Kindness
27. Patience
28. Encouragement
29. Open
30. Order.

End of month reflections for April 2010

Have much tenderness and love toward yourself. The goodness in you comes from God, your Father. When you fail, seek the Lord's forgiveness. Rejoice in your many blessings. Listen with your heart, when others are talking. Be at peace with whatever your current circumstances may be. Know that all is well and God is in control.

Simplify your life. Share more joy. Live faithfully, trusting your dear friends to do what they can. Show gentle encouragement to people who are struggling. Share the good news of our loving God. To be a good friend, let the Holy Spirit guide you in the way of kindness. Trust others. Have patience, keep the faith, and keep a spirit of encouragement. By being open and loving, God can and will make a way when there seems to be no way. Maintain order in your life. Be a joyful, dear friend.

Words for May 2010

1. Humility
2. Something beautiful
3. Light
4. Peace
5. Joy
6. Friendship
7. Blessings
8. Faithfulness
9. Be at peace
10. Casually
11. Faith
12. Be kind
13. Love
14. Tenderness
15. Thankful heart
16. Health
17. Perseverance
18. God is in control
19. God is present
20. Courage
21. Strength
22. Do right
23. Holy Spirit
24. Treasure
25. Be holy
26. Truth
27. Light
28. Goodness
29. Praise the Lord
30. Father, Son, and Holy Spirit
31. Love.

End of month reflections for May 2010

It is okay to have humility, to humble yourself. Allow God to make something beautiful of your life. Let in the light of his love. God is in control. Be at peace because God is present. Share your joy and your courage with the friendships that mean the most to you. You gain strength and blessings when you do what is right.

Because of the faithfulness of the Holy Spirit, you can be at peace. Treasure your friendships. Casually live your life being holy. Have a great faith. Live in truth, being kindhearted. Let your light shine with goodness and tenderness toward others. Praise the Lord with a thankful heart. Praise the Father, Son, and Holy Spirit. Health, well-being, and love are connected. So keep love central in your life.

Words for June 2010

1. Joy
2. Goodness
3. Love
4. Beautiful
5. Listen
6. Angel
7. Wisdom
8. Shine
9. Joy
10. Faithful work
11. Heart of Jesus
12. Pure heart
13. Trust
14. Helpful
15. Goodness
16. Quietly
17. Encourage
18. Shine
19. Trust in God
20. Courage
21. Joy of the Lord
22. Journey
23. Rest
24. Quiet
25. Spirit of God
26. Healing
27. Spirit of love
28. God's grace
29. Give thanks
30. Speak the truth.

End of month reflections for June 2010

Live a joy filled life. Let your light shine through the goodness within you. Trust in God's love. Have the courage to live a beautiful life. The joy of the Lord is your strength. Listen carefully to God's word on your life journey.

The angels of God watch over your life. Rest and be at peace in the ancient wisdom of the saints. As you live a quiet peaceful life, God's light will shine through. The spirit of God will bring joy and healing.

Do your work faithfully in a spirit of love. Let the heart of Jesus and God's amazing grace embrace your life. Keep your heart pure and open. Give thanks for your life and the love that is yours. Trust God to lead you as you speak the truth in love. Be helpful and kind. Let your goodness, quietly encourage others on the journey of life.

Words for July 2010

1. Healing
2. Listen
3. Smile
4. Courage
5. Be kind
6. Loved
7. Spirit of guidance
8. Spiritual journey
9. Words of love
10. Angels
11. All is well
12. Follow Jesus
13. Hope
14. Praise the Lord
15. Enjoy
16. Mercy
17. Guide
18. Listen
19. Humble
20. Good
21. Keep it simple
22. Seek the Lord
23. Do right
24. Listen to the Lord
25. Seek the Lord
26. Keep the faith
27. Peace of the Lord
28. Something beautiful
29. Faith and grace
30. Be blessed
31. Seek the Lord.

End of month reflections for July 2010

To receive the Lord's healing, you must listen closely to his words written in Sacred Scripture. You must listen with your heart. Humble yourself to the loving smile and goodness of the Lord. You will receive courage from God's word. Keep your life simple. Pay your bills, get out of debt. "Owe no one."

Be kind to others. Seek the Lord with a thankful heart. Know that you are loved. Learn to do right by taking the time to be open to the spirit of God's guidance. Listen to the Lord. You are on a spiritual journey. Seek the Lord by reading his words.

When bad things happen, keep the faith. God's angels and his peace are with you. Know that all is well. God is making something very beautiful of your life. Keep following Jesus. Live a life of faith and grace. Hope in the Lord. Be blessed, praising the Lord. Enjoy God's blessing. Show mercy to others. Keep seeking the Lord. Let him be your guide. Live life well.

Words for August 2010

1. Thank you, Lord
2. Safe place
3. Commitment
4. Safety
5. Healing
6. Quiet time
7. Faith
8. Courage
9. Rest
10. Generous
11. Friend
12. Kindness
13. Forgive
14. Love
15. Little
16. Rest
17. Sunshine
18. Listen
19. Praise the Lord
20. Little one
21. True
22. Trust
23. Endure
24. Friend
25. Be present
26. Be good
27. Kindness
28. Joy
29. Jesus
30. Holiness
31. God's presence.

End of month reflections for August 2010

Thank you, Lord, for the sunshine and a safe place to be and to listen to you. Help me with my commitment to sing praise to you. I know that there is safety in being your little one. There is true healing to be found in spending time in your presence. I trust in your faithfulness, as I endure the challenges of daily life. I find courage in the love and support of friends and family.

Help me to rest and be present to others, to be generous and a good friend. Help me to show kindness even when kindness has not been shown to me. Help me to be full of joy, to forgive as Jesus forgives, to love and to be holy in my little way. I trust in God's presence.

Words for September 2010

1. Faith
2. Give thanks
3. Change
4. Humble
5. Wisdom of heart
6. Faithful
7. Lead me
8. Walk in God's love
9. Joy
10. Help me
11. Peace of the Lord
12. Guide me
13. Something beautiful
14. Freedom
15. Quiet
16. Peace
17. Be calm
18. All is well
19. Rest
20. Joyful heart
21. Great is thy faithfulness
22. God is God
23. Do right
24. Wisdom
25. Quiet heart
26. Rest
27. Keep it simple
28. Come Holy Spirit
29. Angels
30. Peace of the Lord.

End of month reflections for September 2010

To have great faith, take time to rest in the Lord's presence. Give him thanks with a joyful heart. Change your negative attitude by realizing God's faithfulness. It keeps you humble to know that God is God. He is in control. Seek his wisdom with your whole heart. Do right and be faithful.

Wisdom comes as you seek a quiet heart, walk in God's love and rest in his presence. There is joy to be found in keeping life simple. Find time to rest and to just be. The Holy Spirit gives peace of soul. God's holy angels guide and protect, helping you to make right choices. God can make something beautiful of your life. The peace of the Lord brings freedom to live life well.

Words for October 2010

1. God is on our side
2. Guardian angels
3. Calm
4. Wisdom
5. Breathe
6. Faithfulness
7. Trust
8. Hope
9. Be kind
10. Give thanks
11. Blessings
12. Be faithful
13. Holy Spirit
14. Truth
15. Light
16. Joy
17. Persistence
18. Humble
19. Listen
20. Endurance
21. Courage
22. Wait
23. The best
24. Forgiveness
25. Love
26. Something beautiful
27. Goodness
28. All is well
29. Do good
30. Christ like
31. Holy angels.

End of month reflections for October 2010

Regardless of what is going on in our life, God is on our side. He sends guardian angels to guide and protect. Remain calm and be a humble servant. We gain wisdom when we listen carefully to the concerns of others. Remember to breathe deeply when enduring any hardship. Trust in God's faithfulness. Be of good courage. Trust and wait in hope for the best plan God has for your life.

Be kind and seek forgiveness when you fail. Give thanks, give love, and give blessings. Let God make something beautiful of your life. Be a faithful follower. Let God's goodness and the Holy Spirit guide your actions. All is well when you seek the truth. Seek to do good deeds. Be a light in the dark places. Be Christ like. Share the joy of the Holy Angels. Persistence is needed in doing good.

Words for November 2010

1. Deeper faith
2. Give
3. Strength
4. Jesus
5. Comfort
6. Goodness
7. Lead me
8. Peace
9. Be kind
10. Faith
11. Trust
12. Simple
13. Obey
14. Perseverance
15. Love
16. Gentleness
17. Quiet lives
18. Shine
19. Listen
20. God's plan
21. Humor
22. Simple
23. Hope
24. Remember
25. Give
26. Calm
27. Be real
28. Be joyful
29. Hope
30. Surrender.

End of month reflections for November 2010

Lord, I want a deeper faith. I want my light to shine. Please give me a heart that will listen to the promptings of the Holy Spirit. Give me the strength I need to follow God's plan, with Jesus as my guide. Give me a good sense of humor and great hope. Help me to give comfort with simple goodness. Lead me moment by moment. Help me remember your love.

I pray for peace in my heart. I give thanks to you, Lord, for all your blessings. Help me to be kind and calm with others. Thank you for the gift of faith. Help me to be real and to trust in your plan for my life. Help me to be a joyful person, keeping my life simple and hopeful. Help me to obey your will, to completely surrender to the love that you have in store for my life.

Words for December 2010

1. Safe	12. Goodness	23. Silence
2. Trust	13. Walk	24. Positive
3. Be joyful	14. Simple	25. Simple
4. Journey	15. Joy	26. Listen
5. Pray	16. Faith	27. Hope
6. Forgiveness	17. Keep on	28. Faithful God
7. God alone	18. Goodness	29. Do right
8. Encourage	19. Balance	30. Humor
9. Be not afraid	20. Love	31. Jesus.
10. Wise	21. Hopeful	
11. Calm	22. Humble	

End of month reflections for December 2010

Keep us safe, Lord, till the storms pass. We trust in your goodness to help keep balance in life. Help us to be joyful and to love deeply on this journey. Keep us hopeful of brighter days. We pray with a humble spirit, seeking forgiveness of our sins.

Wait in silence for God to deliver from weaknesses. Stay positive, encourage others, and keep life simple. Do not be afraid. Listen to wise counsel. Hope can be renewed by creating a calmness of the soul and trusting in our faithful God. His love and goodness sustains us. Always do your best to do what is right. Walk humbly in the presence of God. Keep a sense of humor. Let Jesus be your guide in sharing the spirit of God's gift of faith. Surrender your will and life to God.

2011

Words for January 2011

1. Humble heart
2. Kindness
3. Jesus
4. Praise the Lord
5. The Love of God
6. Love and Sunshine
7. Listen
8. Wisdom
9. Encourage
10. Deep faith
11. Trust and obey
12. Be glad
13. Feel
14. Protection
15. Relax
16. Joy
17. Surrender
18. Blessings
19. Open Heart
20. Do right
21. Be calm
22. Thank you Lord
23. Be at peace
24. All is well
25. Keep the faith
26. Be calm
27. Be not afraid
28. Safe place
29. All is well
30. Joy
31. Strength.

End of month reflections for January 2011

Surrender your life to God with a humble heart. His wisdom and loving kindness show through his son, Jesus. Praise the Lord. The love of God endures forever. Let his love and sunshine flow freely through your life. In the quietness of your heart, listen carefully to gain wisdom. Encourage others to trust and obey the Lord's commandments. Be glad and enjoy the Lord. Feel his loving protection. Take time to relax in his presence. Joy will come back to you when you surrender your life to God. His blessings will flow into your open heart.

Keep life simple by doing what is right. You can be calm in the midst of the storms. Thank the Lord for the peace that comes knowing all is well. Keep the faith. Do not be afraid. You are in the safe place of God's loving presence. Joy and strength comes from the Lord.

Words for February 2011

1. Faith
2. Open heart
3. Open heart
4. Love
5. Hope
6. Shine
7. Goodness
8. Trust
9. Goodness
10. Speak from the heart
11. Comfort
12. Blessings
13. Faithfulness
14. Patience
15. Inspiration
16. Lead me
17. Goodness
18. Quiet place
19. Love and laughter
20. Respect
21. Keep calm
22. Trust and obey
23. Wisdom
24. Kindness
25. Friendship
26. Faith
27. All is well
28. With love.

End of month reflections for February 2011

A deep faith is your guide to goodness. Keep your heart open as you set in a quiet place. An open heart allows you the freedom of love and laughter.

Love and respect is essential to your growth. Keep hope alive for a better tomorrow. Keep a calm spirit. Let your light shine. Keep trusting and obeying God's laws. The goodness and wisdom that comes from a trusting spirit and obeying God's laws will also be a guide for others. Surely kindness, goodness, and deep friendship will follow you all the days of your life.

When dealing with others, speak from the heart giving comfort to their spirit. Let the faith of others be a blessing to your spirit. Know that all is well. God's faithfulness is everlasting. Have much patience with others shortcomings. Speak with love and respect. Be an inspiration.

Words for March 2011

1. Let go
2. Strength
3. Speak with truth
4. Tender love
5. Listen
6. Laugh
7. Courage
8. Listen
9. Light
10. Carry on
11. Joy
12. Pray
13. Faithful
14. God's way
15. Blessings
16. Peace of the Lord
17. Trust
18. Little
19. Blessings
20. Goodness
21. God's mercy
22. Joy
23. Faithfulness
24. Do right
25. Yes Lord
26. All is well
27. Open heart
28. Truth
29. Joy
30. Inspire
31. Love and laugh.

End of month reflections for March 2011

Learn to let go of your fears and trust in the Lord. His strength will magnify your love. Speak the truth with tender love. Abundant blessings await your listening heart. Embrace all goodness with much love and deep laughter. Speak God's mercy and show mercy to others. Accept with courage the person you are in Christ. Be full of joy.

Listen and learn and let God's faithfulness light your path. Do what is right. Carry on day to day by saying yes to the Lord's will with a joyful heart. All is well as you pray with an open heart. Speak the truth and remain faithful to God. Joy and great blessings await and will inspire others. God's peace brings a smile to the hearts of all. Share the love and share the laughter.

Words for April 2011

1. Loving God
2. Sincerity
3. God's will
4. Cheer up
5. Open heart
6. Peace
7. Give thanks
8. Praise the Lord
9. Mercy
10. Laugh
11. Humility
12. Patience
13. Be true
14. Be kind
15. All is well
16. Peace
17. Faith
18. Watch you step
19. Forgiveness
20. Goodness
21. Open
22. Grace
23. Silence
24. Faith
25. Little
26. Rest
27. Calm
28. Praise the Lord
29. Balance
30. Sunshine.

End of month reflections for April 2011

Loving God is the key to loving each other. Use sincerity of heart and actions when dealing with others. Watch your step and don't cross any boundaries. Seek God's will. When you do wrong (and you will) ask for forgiveness. Then cheer up, open your heart to a peaceful solution.

Be gracious; give thanks even when you are disturbed about something. Seek silence to praise the Lord. Ask for the faith and mercy to let the little things go. Don't worry over the small things. Do the best you can and let go. Let God take care of the things you can't.

Laugh a lot, rest often, keep a humble quiet spirit. Have patience with yourself. Don't rush to speak to quickly. Keep the Sabbath holy, praise the Lord, daily. Be true to yourself. Do what is right. Live a balanced life. Be a kind person. Let the sunshine of your heart be known.

Words for May 2011

1. Openness to the Holy Spirit
2. Praise the Lord
3. Give
4. Holy Spirit
5. Be glad
6. Blessings
7. Be not afraid
8. Treasures
9. Calm
10. Friendship
11. Kindness
12. Sunshine
13. Encourage
14. Love
15. Listen
16. Faith
17. Joy
18. Peace
19. Pray
20. Strength
21. Be at peace
22. Friendship
23. Love
24. Be at peace
25. Do right
26. Goodness
27. Love
28. Smile
29. Hope
30. Truth
31. Treasure.

End of month reflections for May 2011

The key to peace of mind and heart is openness to the Holy Spirit. Sing your praise to the Lord. Keep joy in your heart. Give your heart to the Lord and peace will flow from the gift of the Holy Spirit. Pray for a deeper understanding of God's call on your life. Blessings will flow in as you bless others. Be at peace because all is well. Do not be afraid.

Friendships are a great treasure of love. Keep calm and do right. Show kindness. Goodness and the sunshine of God's love is an encouragement to others. Smile big, love huge, and live in hope for a better tomorrow.

Listen closely and you will hear the truth. Your faith is to be treasured. Nurture your faith by reading and studying God's word.

Words for June 2011

1. Listen
2. God's plan
3. Faithful
4. Courage
5. Angels
6. Remain faithful
7. Jesus
8. Do right
9. Trust
10. Love
11. Remain faithful
12. Peace
13. Lift up
14. Be nice
15. Joy
16. A dear friend
17. Healing
18. Be present
19. Simple
20. Listen
21. Joyful
22. Goodness
23. Rest
24. Compassion
25. Friendship
26. Shine
27. Time to heal
28. Wisdom
29. Keep the faith
30. Pray and trust.

End of month reflections for June 2011

To receive the healing you need, listen to the Lord's call on your life. God's plan for you is directed by being present to the moment. Don't focus on yesterday. Live today. Be faithful to God, family, friends and work. It is that simple. Take courage because you are learning to listen. The angels are protecting. Have a joyful spirit as you remain faithful. See the goodness of others who trust Jesus as their savior.

You will get the rest you need when you do what is right. Peaceful sleep will come. Have a heart of compassion for those who fall. Remember your own weaknesses. Trust the Lord to help right the wrongs. Appreciate the blessing of friendships and love. Their light shines in your life and makes you a better person. Remain faithful to them. It is time to forgive. It is time to heal. Be at peace as you seek wisdom. Lift up in prayer all those who have a wounded spirit. Help them to keep the faith. Be nice to them, pray for them. Be a spirit of love and joy. Be a dear friend. Trust the Lord.

Words for July 2011

1. Live in the light of God's love
2. Safe
3. Rest
4. Trust
5. Hope
6. Goodness
7. Wait
8. Keep hope alive
9. Listen
10. Help
11. Forgiveness
12. Don't be afraid
13. Kindness
14. Praise the Lord
15. Love
16. Trust
17. Listen
18. God
19. Joy
20. Be faithful
21. Thank you
22. Shine
23. Peace
24. Wisdom
25. Helpful
26. Respect
27. Bless
28. Peace
29. Joy
30. Courage
31. Give thanks.

End of month reflections for July 2011

Live in the light of God's love. You are safe in the loving arms of God. You can be at peace as you rest in his presence. Joyfully accept and trust God's faithfulness. Be true to God. Hope always and remember to say thank you for the goodness you have received.

Count your blessings. Let your light shine. Wait patiently. Be at peace as you keep hope alive. Seek wisdom, learn from mistakes. Listen to the voice of reason. Be helpful when you can. Seek help when you need it. Show respect for others. Seek forgiveness and bless others. Don't be afraid. God has a plan. Be at peace by showing kindness and joy. Sing your praise to the Lord. Have courage in difficult times. God will see you through.

Words for August 2011

1. Simple
2. Courage
3. Faithful
4. God's presence
5. All is well
6. Be still
7. Rest
8. Trust
9. Peace
10. Angels
11. Little
12. Quiet
13. Goodness
14. Faithfulness
15. Joy
16. Rest
17. Sunshine
18. Surrender
19. Be a peace
20. Love
21. Joy
22. Faithful
23. Be nice
24. Lead me
25. Silence
26. Smile
27. Quiet
28. Angels
29. Open
30. God's goodness
31. Support.

End of month reflections for August 2011

Live a good, wholesome, simple life. Things are a lot easier if we keep life simple. It takes courage to honor simplicity. We must surrender to the Lord's guidance. We must be faithful to our commitment to God. We can be at peace in God's loving presence. We can believe that all is well. Be a joyful witness to God's love. Take the time to be still, be faithful, and rest in the Lord's presence. Be nice to others regardless of the circumstances. Trust God to lead to peace in following his commands.

Many times silence is the best response. Silence can speak volumes. We can let the angels do their work as we set in silence and just smile. The little that we have to do while being quiet, can work wonders. The angels will work to allow the goodness in others to open their hearts to God's faithfulness.

If we can open our hearts to God's goodness, we will find joy and support for our lives. Rest in God's light. Jesus Christ, the Son of the Living God, we believe.

Words for September 2011

1. Love
2. Peace of the Lord
3. Surrender
4. Wisdom
5. Hope
6. Listen
7. Safe place
8. Simple
9. Joy
10. Listen
11. Forgive
12. Mary
13. Jesus
14. Believe
15. Open heart
16. Be calm
17. Keep the faith
18. Generous
19. Joy
20. Faithful
21. Praise the Lord
22. Open heart
23. God our Father
24. All is well
25. Rest
26. Serve the Lord
27. The power of Love
28. Walk with God
29. Angels
30. Listen.

End of month reflections for September 2011

Love is on the rise so be generous in giving and receiving. The peace of the Lord brings joy to your spirit as you surrender your will to his. Keep ever faithful to the wisdom of the ages. Sing your praise to the Lord who always gives hope as you look to the future. Keep your heart open as you listen to the spirit of God our Father.

God is your safe place to rest and know that all is well. Keep your life simple. Take the time to rest in God's loving presence. Let joy shine in your life as your serve the Lord. Listen to his words and know the power of love. Keep a forgiving spirit as you walk with God. Call on the intercessions of the Blessed Virgin Mary, the Mother of God, Jesus the beloved Son of God and all the angels and saints, your family and friends to help you in your needs. Listen and know that they are all on your side. Listen to the Spirits call and believe with a trusting open heart that your prayers are heard.

When storms come, do your best to remain calm. Keep the faith. Know that you always have the Lord's help. Keep trusting that all is well. Rest your faith in the power of love. Serve the Lord with gladness.

Words for October 2011

1. Protection
2. Yield
3. The love of God
4. Friend
5. All is well
6. Hold on
7. Trust
8. Courage
9. Keep the faith
10. Keep it simple
11. Do right
12. Mercy
13. Praise the Lord
14. Loved
15. Faithful
16. Sunshine
17. Safe
18. Surrender
19. Listen
20. Goodness
21. Embrace the day
22. Shine
23. Respect
24. Open heart
25. Guide us
26. Listen
27. Treasures
28. Angels
29. Gifts
30. All is well
31. For all the saints.

End of month reflections for October 2011

Stop all worry. You are under the protection of the Most High God. You are safe in his loving care. Yield in total surrender to his love. Listen carefully to your friends. Trust in their goodness and know that all is well.

Embrace each new day and hold on to the sunshine in your life. Trust and respect the courage of an open heart. Keep the faith. Seek the Lord's guidance. Keep everything simple. Show respect as you listen carefully and wait patiently for the answers you need. Respect others and do what is right. Life is full of treasures and God's mercy.

Join with all the saints and angels singing praise to the Lord. Accept the gifts of friendship. Know that you are loved. All is still well. Be a faithful witness of God's love. Give thanks for all the saints who let their light shine. Be sunshine for others.

LINDA F. STAFFORD

Words for November 2011

1. Thanks
2. Wisdom
3. God will provide
4. Goodness
5. Work
6. Hope
7. Courage
8. Keep loving
9. Wonderful
10. Seek wisdom
11. Trust
12. Safe
13. Praise the Lord
14. Listen
15. Walk with God
16. Believe
17. God's peace
18. Open heart
19. Open my heart
20. Tenderness
21. God is love
22. Love
23. Grace
24. Pray for me
25. Rest and peace
26. See the beauty and goodness
27. Hope
28. Surrender
29. Faithful
30. Joy of the Lord.

End of month reflections for November 2011

A prayer:

Thank you, Lord, for your love. Please keep my heart open to the wisdom that comes from having an open heart. Lord, I know you will provide all the tenderness and goodness I need because you, Lord, are love. I know that I must continue to work and love and keep hope alive. I know your grace will give me the courage to follow what is right. I need others to continue to pray for me, and to keep a loving heart toward me. Thank you, Lord, for the days of rest and peace.

It is wonderful to see the beauty and goodness that come when I seek your will and wisdom. You give me hope for the future. I trust and I surrender my life to you. I know that I am safe in your great faithfulness. I praise you, Lord, with a joyful open heart. I listen to your will as I walk with you. I do believe in you. I trust you for your peace. Love, your "little" Linda.

Words for December 2011

1. Blessings
2. Special
3. Healing
4. Goodness
5. Kindness
6. Be grateful
7. Compassion
8. All is well
9. Encouragement
10. Understanding
11. Pray
12. Goodness
13. Guidance
14. Little
15. Simple
16. Do right
17. Respect
18. Angels
19. Listen
20. Light
21. Lord of the moments
22. Jesus
23. Encouragement
24. Gentle
25. Praise
26. Respect
27. Be present
28. Love
29. Faithful
30. Thank you Lord
31. Jesus.

End of month reflections for December 2011

The blessings of the Lord are many and are to be respected. You are very special to God. So much so that he has angels watching over and protecting you. God's healing love is shown through others. Listen to the goodness around you. Let Christ's light shine through all you do by showing kindness with the Lord of the moments as your guide. Be forever grateful to Jesus your savior. His compassion and encouragement is also shown through others. Know that all is well as you live each day guided by God's gentle hand. He is the encouragement you will receive. Praise God. Seek understanding and respect for others by and through prayers.

Be present to others. It is important to let goodness be your guide and let love be your motive. Be open to the guidance of the Holy Spirit. God is faithful. Be faithful to God. Know that little is so much more when God is in it. Thank you, Lord. Keep your life simple. Trust Jesus and do what is right. Praise the Lord! Words are gifts from God.

"You will be given at that moment what you are to say" (Mat. 10:19).

"When your heart speaks, take good notes" (Judith Cambell).

2012

I believe in God. Every day I will get up praising God. Thanking God for the gift of faith and the gift of life. My purpose is to live in the presence of God. I start my day with a good cup of coffee-praying, reading, and reflecting. I will "do right." I believe that God's Spirit will guide me if I open myself to his presence. I will open my heart to what others are feeling. I will be a kinder presence. I will live my faith, knowing that God is in control. I trust God. He loves me. I love Him. All will be well!

Words for January 2012

1. Listen
2. Encourage
3. God loves us
4. God cares/provides
5. Honest
6. Light of God
7. God Cares
8. Angel
9. Be calm
10. The presence of God
11. God is Faithful/trust Him
12. Thank you Lord
13. Angels of God
14. Respect
15. God's Favor
16. Relax
17. Love and Trust
18. Faith
19. Joy
20. Blessings
21. Rest in God
22. Open Heart
23. Blessings
24. Encourage
25. God is faithful
26. Generous God
27. Bloom where planted
28. Healing
29. Divine Love of God
30. Very quiet
31. Relax

End of month reflections for January 2012

Listen to your heart. You can love and trust people to do right. Encourage people to strengthen their faith. Let people know that God loves us. Spread joy to others by expressing the fact that God cares. He provides what we need. Surrender your life to God. Be honest with him. Find rest in the light of God's love.

When we open our heart to God, we realize that he cares. His blessings are all around. His angels encourage us on our life journey. Be calm, God is faithful. Take time to rest in the presence of Almighty God.

God is a generous God. God is always faithful, trust Him. Bloom exactly where you are planted. Thank you, Lord, for your healing love. Angels of God protect us. Angels of God guide us.

The divine love of God is to be respected. Accept his unfailing love. Be very quiet before the Lord. Allow God's favor to rest on your life. Relax, all is well. Let the light of your faith shine so that it will radiate to the hearts of others.

Words for February 2012

1. Goodness
2. Peace
3. Be encouraging
4. Wisdom
5. Light
6. God is Good
7. Kindness
8. Accept God's goodness
9. Wait
10. God is good and merciful
11. God's wisdom
12. Protect
13. God's love
14. Respect
15. Surrender
16. God cares
17. Silence
18. Simple
19. Encouragement
20. Joyful
21. Follow Jesus
22. Best Friend
23. Be kindhearted
24. Our Father
25. Listen
26. Angels
27. God's love
28. Respect

End of month reflections for February 2012

God's goodness surrounds us as we surrender all to Him. The peace of knowing that God cares for us is encouraging. We will do our best to live life with much love and laughter. Seek God's wisdom, surrendering all of life to him.

His light guides us as we set in prayerful silence. God is good. Do the best to keep life simple. Show kindness to others. Continue to give encouragement to people. Accept God's goodness. Be joyful, rejoicing in the Lord. Affectionately follow Jesus by accepting his healing and his forgiveness when we fail. He is our best friend. Enjoy time waiting in God's presence. He teaches us to be kindhearted. God is good and merciful. He is our father. Learn of God's wisdom by reading his word, by listening to his heart. He sends his angels to protect. God's love is amazing. We bow our heart in respect and praise.

Words for March 2012

1. Everything is going to be all right
2. Live a holy life
3. Honest
4. God's light
5. Lead me
6. Laughter
7. Goodness
8. Keep it simple
9. God's grace
10. TYL/Thank you, Lord
11. Love and Laughter
12. God is trustworthy
13. Hope
14. Grace
15. Listen
16. Be quiet
17. Trust the Lord
18. Rejoice
19. All is well
20. Holy Spirit
21. Be kind
22. God's light
23. TYL/Thank you, Lord
24. Be open
25. Love and laugh
26. Keep the Faith
27. God's Love
28. Obedience
29. Make a difference
30. Joyful
31. Wholeheartedly

End of month reflections for March 2012

No matter what happens, everything is going to be all right. The best thing to do is to keep living a holy life, rejoicing in the Lord. Keep yourself honest before all, believing that all is well. Be open to God's light through the power of the Holy Spirit. The Holy Spirit will lead you in the way that you should live. Always be kind to others. Share much laughter with everyone. Let God's light be your focus. See the goodness in all you encounter. Remember to say (TYL) Thank You, Lord, for your goodness.

Be open to God's grace by avoiding distractions. Keep your life simple. Keep on loving the people that share in your journey to heaven. Laughter is vital to your soul. (TYL) Thank You, Lord, for the laughter.

We cherish the gift of our faith. We want to share our love and devotion for you by being obedient to your word. Help us to keep hope alive letting our life make a difference. God's grace is abundant. Be joyful in the Lord. Listen carefully to His call on your life. Be quiet before God. Trust wholeheartedly in the Lord.

Words for April 2012

1. God's strength
2. God's blessings
3. Call on the Lord
4. Divine power
5. God's presence
6. Live a Spiritual life
7. Know God better
8. Be humble
9. Submit to the Holy Spirit
10. Do right
11. Keep an open heart
12. Repent of wrongs
13. See the goodness in others
14. Believe in goodness
15. Divine Mercy
16. Be open to the Holy Spirit
17. Be a quiet model
18. Show joy
19. Raise your face to God
20. Expect the good
21. Don't be afraid
22. Listen better
23. The gift of faith
24. God takes care
25. Surrender to God
26. Encouragement
27. Faithful
28. Quiet seeking
29. Child of God
30. Sunshine

End of month reflections for April 2012

God's strength will sustain you. Raise your face to his loving embrace. Accept his blessings. Expect the goodness of the Lord. Just call on him. Do not be afraid. God's divine power is always in control. Learn to listen better in God's presence.

Accept the gift of faith with an open heart. Live a spiritual life, knowing that God will take care. Get to know God better by surrendering your life to his loving hands. Be humble, not proud. Be an inspiration. Be a person of encouragement to others. Submit to the Holy Spirit's guidance. Do what is right by being faithful. Keep an open heart, quietly seeking God's will.

Repent of wrongs and move on with life. You are a child of God. Seek and believe in the goodness in others. Let the sunshine of Divine Mercy be reflected in your life. Be open to the Holy Spirit. Be a quiet model, showing a joyful presence.

Words for May 2012

1. All is well
2. The light of God's Love
3. Know God
4. Lighten up
5. Love from the heart
6. Let go
7. Trust God
8. God's peace
9. Smile
10. Find joy today
11. Be at peace
12. Be open to God's Plan
13. Care
14. Peaceful
15. It is love that saves
16. Quiet peace
17. God's perfect plan
18. Be joyful
19. Rest
20. Help me, Lord!
21. Friendship
22. Thank you for your faithfulness
23. Hard work and service
24. God's will
25. Be faithful
26. Slow down
27. Smile
28. Hope
29. Holy Spirit
30. Patience
31. Honor and respect

End of month reflections for May 2012

No matter what may seem to be wrong in your life, if you place everything in God's loving hands, you can be assured that "all is well." God's perfect plan is in place for your life. Do the best you can in the light of God's love. Be a joyful person. To know God's plan, you must take time for resting in his presence. Let God lighten your heavy load. Ask the Lord for his help. Love from the heart. Be thankful for his faithfulness. Keep trusting God to help you in the hard work and service you give. God's peace flows from seeking and doing God's will.

Keep smiling by being faithful to the Lord's work you are called too. Find joy in today by slowing down. Be at peace with God's loving plan. Keep hope alive. Care deeply about people. Let the Holy Spirit be your guide. Keep a peaceful disposition. Have a lot of patience with yourself. Remember that it is love that saves us. Show honor and respect for people. Keep a quiet peace about yourself.

Words for June 2012

1. Goodness
2. Encourage
3. Love
4. Courage
5. Guarded by angels
6. Help me, Lord
7. Listen to God
8. Respect
9. God's Grace
10. Peace
11. Respect
12. Love and trust
13. Guide me
14. Blessings
15. Treasures
16. Jesus
17. Strength
18. Open heart
19. Thankful
20. Treasures
21. Faithful
22. Joy
23. Open heart
24. Encourage
25. Do right
26. Hope
27. Jesus, "God saves"
28. Continued healing
29. Blessings

End of month reflections for June 2012

The goodness of God gives us strength and encourages us to do better. When we keep our heart open to his love, we have the courage to keep living a faith filled life. Be thankful that we are guarded by his holy angels. We have so many blessings of beautiful treasures in family, friends, co-workers, church, and neighbors. The Lord helps us to do what is right by being faithful to the people in our life. Listen to God to be filled with joy. Respect others when they open their heart, sharing their joys and struggles. It is God's grace that helps us to know to be an encourager.

God's gift of eternal life gives us hope. To live in peace always do what is right. Live in the light of God's glorious sunshine. Because of Jesus, God saves us. Trust in his continual healing as he guides and showers many blessings. God bless you, abundantly.

Words for July 2012

1. Love and laugh
2. Relax
3. Humble
4. Keep it simple
5. Encouraging
6. Mercy
7. Hope
8. Surrender
9. Faithful
10. Listen
11. Quiet place of peace
12. Goodness
13. Do right
14. Encouraged
15. God's plan
16. Whatever happens/trust
17. Peace
18. Simple
19. Rest
20. Respect
21. Praise the Lord
22. Let your light shine
23. Surrender
24. God is faithful
25. Treasure
26. Love and be kind
27. Open heart
28. Do good
29. Be open
30. Faith forward
31. Thankfulness

End of month reflections for July 2012

Jesus, teach us to love and laugh. Help us to find your peace through life's challenges. Give us the free time we need to relax, keeping our life simple. Help us to be humble before you, to rest in your loving presence, respecting all life.

Remind us to keep encouraging each other. We praise you, Lord for your great mercy. We thank you, Lord, for your love. Let your light shine in us. Our hope is in you as we surrender our life to you. God's love is faithful. We treasure your love that helps us to listen to others, to be more loving and kind.

Help us to find a quiet place of peace where we can open our hearts to you. Open our eyes to the goodness around us. Help us to do good deeds of love, to do what is right, to be open to the needs of others.

We are encouraged by your holy word that gives us guidance to keep moving our faith forward. We asked for your help in seeking your plan for the rest of this life journey. With a thankful heart, we trust in your loving faithfulness. We know that whatever happens we must let it unfold with trust and with love.

Words for August 2012

1. Courage
2. Lead
3. Open heart
4. Listen
5. Joy
6. A light of hope
7. All is well
8. Keep the faith
9. Goodness
10. Peace of the Lord
11. Be open to inspiration
12. Encourage
13. Be true
14. Hope
15. Believe
16. Forgive
17. Be still and listen
18. Treasured
19. Do right
20. God's plan
21. Be very kindhearted
22. Open heart
23. Faithful
24. Trust
25. Listen
26. Faithful
27. Encouragement
28. Joyful
29. Jesus
30. Faithful
31. Be at peace

End of month reflections for August 2012

Be of good courage, the Lord is on your side. You are a treasured friend. The Lord is leading you to do right. Keep an open heart to God's loving plan. Listen carefully to his direction to be a very kind hearted, joy filled, loving person.

Keep your heart open to the light of hope, to God's faithfulness. Know that all is well. Keep trusting in God's love. Live your life in the spirit of faith.

Listen to the goodness of other faithful souls. The peace of the Lord is yours when you are an instrument of encouragement. Be open to the inspiration of the Holy Spirit. Let Jesus be your guide. Be true to your faithful friendships and family.

Keep your hope in the Lord's guidance. Be at peace. Believe in the goodness of others. Be quick to forgive. Take time to be still before the Lord. Listen for his directions.

Words for September 2012

1. Be a kind presence
2. Hope
3. Listen carefully
4. Guide
5. Goodness
6. Seek God
7. Encouragement
8. Walk in the light
9. Have an open heart
10. Surrender
11. Respect
12. Blessings of friendship
13. Love
14. Jesus
15. Journey
16. Listen
17. Trust the Lord
18. Love
19. Faithful
20. Peace of the Lord
21. Be joyful
22. Encourage
23. Simplify your life
24. Light
25. Rest
26. Do right
27. Respect
28. Blessing of friendship
29. Trust the Lord
30. It's about listening

LINDA F. STAFFORD

End of month reflections for September 2012

All people go through hard times. Be a kinder presence for them by showing love and respect for who they are and what they do. Be a faithful witness of God's love. Listen carefully to their story, radiating the peace of the Lord. Pray silently, "Guide me, Lord."

Be a joyful person, full of the goodness from God. Encourage all who seek God. It helps to simplify your life. This frees you to be a source of light among your circle. As we walk in the light of God's love, keeping an open heart, we can surrender our life circumstances to him. When we do right by people, loving them, we gain their respect.

Be thankful for the blessings of friendship. Often times, silence is the best response to a conflict. Let the love of Jesus be a guide. Trust the Lord on the journey to heaven.

Life is about listening to God's word. Listen with a heart full of love, trusting in God's message.

Words for October 2012

1. My hope is in the Lord
2. Meek
3. Calm
4. Lord, help me
5. Trust the Lord
6. Let God's light shine
7. God's presence
8. Joyful heart
9. Blessings
10. Respect
11. Faithful
12. Be hopeful
13. Free
14. Goodness
15. Believe
16. Jesus
17. Blessings
18. Compassion
19. Do right
20. Simple
21. Listen
22. Faith
23. Encouragement
24. Today
25. Jesus
26. Humble
27. Acceptance
28. All is well
29. Healing
30. Wait
31. Support

End of month reflections for October 2012

My hope is in the Lord of all. I am a meek soul, who has so many blessings. Thanks to the Lord who has helped me. The Lord guides me to do what is right. I put all my trust in my Jesus.

My life is really quite simple. I need to let God's light shine through all I do. I need to listen carefully to hear God speak words of encouragement. I keep the faith with a joyful heart as God's blessings flow.

I respect all of life. I let Jesus be my guide. I try every day to be a faithful, humble, hopeful person. I have learned to accept what I cannot change. Acceptance frees me to trust that all is well, to work with what I have been given. I let the goodness inside myself, the goodness in others be the healing balm for forgiveness. I wait on the Lord for the support I need. God's timing is always on time. (TYL) Thank you, Lord.

Words for November 2012

1. Joyful
2. Spend
3. Enjoy
4. Calm
5. Encouragement
6. Hope
7. Positive
8. Believe
9. Today
10. It's about love
11. Keep good going
12. Heart
13. Reflect
14. Faith
15. Blessings
16. Give
17. Be nice
18. Help us enjoy the call
19. Praise
20. Thankfulness
21. Jesus
22. Listen
23. Peace
24. Angels
25. All is well
26. Joy
27. Faith
28. God's presence
29. Faith
30. Life choices

End of month reflections for November 2012

Live your life with a joyful spirit. Give of yourself. Spend time in prayer before each event. Be a nice person. Enjoy the company of whoever you are with. Ask the Lord to help you enjoy your work, your mission.

Have a calm presence about yourself. Say often, "I believe in God's loving protection." Be a source of encouragement by praising what others are doing. Hope in the Lord. Have a spirit of thankfulness. Have a positive attitude. Walk with Jesus believing and trusting in his care. Listen to him speaking to your heart. Know that today is the day that the Lord made and be at peace.

Be considerate of all your friendships. When you can't be there for them, send your angel to their angel for support. Life is about love, believing that all is well. Just keep the good going by being a true joy to be around. Listen carefully with your heart. Keep your faith strong. Pray and reflect God's presence. Let your faith be a blessing to all who know you. Love the Lord your God. Put your life choices in his hands.

Words for December 2012

1. Responsibility
2. Humble
3. Kinder
4. Be still
5. Share
6. Respect
7. Mary, Mother of God
8. Surrender
9. Holy Spirit
10. Sheltered
11. Safe
12. Pray
13. Joy
14. Home
15. Listen
16. Faithfulness
17. Plan
18. Sheltered
19. Bless us
20. Good choices
21. Smile
22. Joyful
23. Peace
24. Shelter
25. Others
26. Little
27. Love, laughter, trust, pray
28. Gentle quiet spirit
29. Tenderness
30. Love and goodness
31. Jesus

End of month reflections for December 2012

It is my responsibility to plan for a better life. (Spiritually and financially.) With a humble spirit, I realize that I have always been sheltered in the loving arms of God. I will be kinder, continuing to ask God to bless us. I will be still, seeking God's help to make good choices. I will continue to share a smile, showing respect to others. I will be a more joyful person. I ask Mary, the Mother of God, to pray for me for guidance in the way of peace in my heart as I surrender my life to the shelter of God's love.

I pray for the gift of the Holy Spirit in all our lives. I give thanks that we are all sheltered in God's love. Our little steps day by day, trusting in the Lord will lead to a safe place. Daily duties include: love, laughter, trust, and prayer.

I pray for a gentle, quiet spirit, for the gift of joy and tenderness. I pray that people feel at home around me, to leave my presence with the sense of love and goodness that I see in them. I will listen closely to Jesus's words trusting in God's faithfulness.

> *"The ways of right living people glow with light the longer they live the brighter they shine" (Prov. 4:18).*

> *"Oh, how sweet the light of day, and how wonderful to live in the sunshine! Even if you live a long time, don't take a single day for granted. Take delight in each light filled hour" (Ecc. 11:7–8).*

2013

Words for January 2013

1. Reflect
2. Respect
3. Praise
4. All is well
5. Love
6. Discipline
7. Silence
8. Guidance
9. Be calm
10. Inspire
11. Listen
12. Joy
13. Friends
14. God's Presence
15. Relax
16. Treasure
17. Faithful
18. Listen
19. God's Peace
20. Love
21. Be calm
22. Shelter
23. Riches
24. Believe
25. Protection
26. Bless
27. Today is the Lord's
28. Be patient
29. All is well
30. Goodness
31. Angels

End of month reflections for January 2013

    Take the time to reflect on the gift of the shelters you have. These shelters are God's love embracing us in all of life. Respect the gifts of riches you have received. Gifts of love and friendship and the shelter these provide.

Be a person of praise. Believe in the goodness of others. Keep in mind that whatever happens, God is in control and all will be well. Heavenly protection and love will always bless your life.

Discipline your life with simplicity. Remember that every day is a day the Lord made. There is a time for silence when dealing with difficult situations. Be patient. Seek godly guidance and all will be well. Be calm during stressful activities. Look for the goodness beneath the surface. Inspire others to seek a calm approach. Remember both parties have angels surrounding them. Listen for guidance from the Holy Spirit. Be a person of joy.

It is through true friends that we are aware of God's presence in our lives. We can relax in their presence. Friends are real treasures, forever faithful. They will listen to our concerns. We receive God's peace and love through them as they help to calm our fears. Give thanks to God for your friends. Ask God's blessings on them. Friends help shelter us and add richness to what we believe. They also provide protection by blessing us with their prayers. They remind us that today is the Lord's and he is patient with us. All is well through the goodness of God. He sends his angels to protect and guide.

Words for February 2013

1. Treasure
2. Love
3. Hope
4. Healing
5. Calm
6. Peace
7. Light
8. Wait
9. Quiet place
10. Holy
11. Light
12. Rest
13. Gentle/Kinder Spirit
14. Faith
15. Shelter
16. Closest Friends
17. Gift
18. Be quiet
19. Prayer, love, and laughter
20. Wait in silence
21. Trust
22. Encouragement
23. Do right
24. Listen
25. Joy
26. Do good
27. Be faithful
28. Blessings

LINDA F. STAFFORD

End of month reflections for February 2013

What do you treasure? I treasure love. I have hope for the healing of mind, body, and spirit. I seek the calm that comes with peace by accepting God's light as I wait in a quiet place. God's holy light is found in rest. I can come back to the gentle, kinder spirit of my faith.

I acknowledge the shelter of my closest friends' many gifts of love. There are seasons to be quiet, to be a person of prayer, love, and laughter. It helps to wait in silence. Trust the quiet. Sometimes it is best to just let things be.

We all need encouragement. We all need to do right by each other. Listen carefully to what others say by creating an atmosphere of peaceful joy. We must strive to do good deeds and be faithful. Many blessings are coming our way.

Trouble hearing? Try this:

Truly listen to God . . . turn your inner ear into a place of silent prayer, open your heart to God, walk in his ways and follow the guidance of the Holy Spirit.

Words for March 2013

1. Safe place
2. Jesus
3. Strength
4. See the good
5. Forgive
6. Love and laughter
7. Listen
8. Angels
9. Humble
10. Joy
11. Seek the beauty in life
12. Simple
13. Peace
14. Persistent
15. Strength
16. Hope
17. Forgiveness
18. Goodness
19. Faith
20. Healing
21. All is well
22. Words
23. Holy Spirit
24. The Love of God is faithful
25. All is well
26. Light
27. Joy
28. Blessings
29. Persevere (hold on)
30. Be quiet
31. Rejoice

End of month reflections for March 2013

Thank you, God, for all the safe places you create in my life. Thank you, God, for sending your son, Jesus. Thank you, Lord for the strength I receive from the gifts of the Holy Spirit.

Help me, Father, to see the good that you see. Help me to be a more forgiving person. Help me to shower love and laughter to the people in my life. Help me to listen to the guidance of your angels. Help me to live within my means, to be humble where I need to be. Help me to be a person filled with your joy. Help me to seek and to see the beauty in my life. Help me to keep my life simple and to be at peace with what I cannot change. Help me to be persistent at being a better person.

Give me the strength I need to get through the rough spots that come my way, to be more supportive of others who are going through tough times. Please continue to give me a vision of hope for the future.

Thank you for your forgiveness when I fall short (when I sin.) May the goodness, you created in my heart, overflow with faith and healing.

I know that when I surrender my will to your will that all will be well. Please give me kind words to speak. "Holy Spirit thou art welcome."

I know that the love of God is always faithful and that all is well when I live in the light of God's presence. My heart is overflowing with joy and many blessings. Many more blessings will come into my life.

Lord, continue to help me persevere through the tough times that pop up in this life journey. Help me to hold on to your hand. Help me to keep quiet rather than speaking unkindly. I rejoice in God, my savior. It is Easter. He is risen! He lives!

A quote from Baptist Standard: "You can't spell 'brothers' and not spell 'others.'"

Today's verse: "Keep on loving each other as brothers. Do not forget to entertain strangers, for by so doing some people have entertained angels without knowing it" (Heb. 13:1–2).

LINDA F. STAFFORD

Words for April 2013

1. Hope
2. Blessings
3. Service
4. Open mind/heart
5. Shelter
6. Do right
7. Mercy
8. Faithful
9. Gentleness
10. Courage
11. Discipline
12. Kindness
13. Encourage
14. Shine/Spiritual light
15. All is well
16. Love
17. Thankful
18. Joy is central to faith
19. Listen
20. Be a caring presence
21. Service
22. Hearing God
23. God's Presence
24. Be good
25. Blessings
26. Hope in the Lord
27. Open heart
28. Love one another
29. God is faithful
30. Sunshine

End of month reflections for April 2013

    Never lose hope of the abundant blessings that come with service to others. Keep an open heart and an open mind. Shelter others by doing right by them and showing them mercy. Be faithful in service and gentleness. Pray for the courage and discipline it takes to show kindness in stressful situations.

    Encourage others to let their light shine by being a spiritual light every day. Believe that all is well when showing love. Be a thankful person. Keep joy central to your faith.

    Listen closely and be a caring presence because it has a profound impact on your life and the life of others. Service follows hearing God's voice. His voice is always love. Where God's presence is, there is love.

    Be a good person. Expect many blessings. Keep your hope in the Lord by keeping an open heart and loving one another. God is always faithful. Choose daily to live in the sunshine of his love. Be a happy, loving presence!

Words for May 2013

1. Trust
2. Faith
3. All true love
4. Kindness
5. Blessings
6. Listen
7. Pray
8. Rest
9. Humble
10. Calm
11. Patience
12. All is well
13. Work
14. Shelter
15. Tenderness
16. Guide
17. Healing
18. Peace
19. Safety
20. Truth
21. Faith
22. Goodness
23. Joy
24. Friendship
25. Gentle
26. Spirit
27. Safe
28. Love
29. Respect
30. Do right
31. Friends

End of month reflections words May 2013

Trust God and do what is right. Keep your faith positive. The truth is, all true love is of God. Do your best to show kindness to all. Shower the blessings of respect for others by listening to their concerns. Pray for those concerns. Rest assured in God's loving presence.

Be humble about your own business. Keep a calm disposition. Have patience with yourself. Even though you may be going through a difficult time, realize that all will be well in God's time.

Enjoy the work at hand because it is your present shelter. Show tenderness to the troubled souls you encounter. Let the Holy Spirit be your guide. Healing and peace comes through a caring heart. There is safety in truth and in faith. The goodness and joy of true friendship will bless your life's journey. Keep a gentle spirit and be a safe place for others to share their concerns. Always show love and respect and do right by your friends. Love God, love each other.

LINDA F. STAFFORD

Words for June 2013

1. Respect
2. Journey
3. Love
4. Courage
5. Listen
6. Loving God/ Loving each other
7. Treasures
8. Faith
9. Trust
10. Blessed
11. Encouragement
12. Faithful
13. Love
14. Shelter
15. I am blessed
16. Rest
17. Jesus
18. Wait
19. Treasure
20. All is well
21. Faithfulness
22. Free
23. Deep joy
24. Security
25. Friendship
26. Thankfulness
27. Hope
28. Trust
29. Blessings
30. Journey

End of month reflections words June 2013

Listen carefully:

Learn to respect your life's journey by always keeping love as your goal. Have the courage to listen carefully to our loving God. Be aware of his great care for us.

We must walk this journey together loving each other and gratefully accepting the treasures of family, friendships, and faith. Trust in these treasures. Know that you are blessed. Be a form of encouragement and a faithful presence. Show love and be a safe shelter for others to share their hurts.

We realize that we are blessed when we rest in Jesus's presence. When we wait in silence, we come to know that we are also a treasure. We learn to trust that all is well when we trust in the faithfulness of family, friends, neighbors, and co-workers. Our spirits are free to express the deep joy and security of all our friendships. We have a heart full of thankfulness, hope, and trust of the many blessings yet to be experienced on this journey toward heaven.

Words for July 2013

1. Help me Lord
2. Faith
3. Spirit
4. Simple
5. Silence
6. Peace
7. Healing
8. Courage
9. Joy
10. Shelter
11. Treasures
12. Trust
13. Goodness
14. Love
15. Secured
16. Safe place
17. God's plan
18. Rest
19. Joy
20. Simple
21. Praise
22. Shine
23. Peace
24. God's presence
25. Cherished
26. Appreciate
27. Beautiful
28. Goodness
29. Pray
30. Kindness
31. Grateful

End of month reflections for July 2013

Help me, Lord, to keep the faith and Holy Spirit I received and accepted as gifts from you. Help me to keep my life simple and uncluttered. Help me to seek silence when I need your peace and healing. Please give me the courage I need to face the challenges that life brings. Give me a heart full of joy and thankfulness for your sheltering love.

I thank you for the treasures you have given me. I trust in your love and mercy. I pray that you lead me along the path to goodness and love. I am thankful that I have secured a safe place in your plan for my life. I rest in joy and peace.

Help me to enjoy the simple events of life. I praise you, Lord, and thank you for the sunshine and peace you give. As I seek your presence, Lord, I know that I am cherished. I appreciate these beautiful friendships, the goodness they bring to my life. I pray for them. I am grateful for their kindnesses.

Words for August 2013

Road trip with friend, Pat Farley, was a special spiritual journey. We chose two words to describe the trip. Pat's word was *marvelous*, my word was *wonderful*. There were beautiful sights and insights along this journey.

1. Spiritual journey
2. Blessings
3. Joyfully
4. Surrender
5. Thankful
6. Quiet
7. Hope
8. Trust
9. Moment
10. Peace
11. Faith
12. Love
13. Inspiration
14. Wisdom
15. Two souls
16. Little flowers
17. Respect
18. Surrender
19. Follow Jesus
20. Kindness
21. Wonderful and Marvelous
22. Goodness
23. Plan
24. Joy
25. Encourage
26. Grace
27. Quietness
28. Service
29. Listen
30. Give
31. Faithfulness

End of month reflections for August 2013

Be open to the spiritual journey and the blessings you are receiving. Joyfully surrender with a thankful heart to God's marvelous expressions of love and life.

Be at peace with the quiet hope and trust for the future. Enjoy and share the moments given to you. Keep the faith, go to church. Receive the love, inspiration and wisdom from friendship (two souls and God.) Friendships are little flowers that continually bloom and grow when watered with respect and love.

Surrender your life, following Jesus by living the life you are called to live, loving God and loving each other. Show great kindness to people. Wonderful and marvelous are the days of your life if you are open to the moments. Surely goodness and mercy are part of God's loving plan for your life. Be open to the joys of life. Encourage others who are struggling. Let them know that God's marvelous grace is sufficient. Have a peaceful quietness in your service to others. Listen carefully to what others are saying. Let the service you give be from your heart. Accept and know God's wonderful faithfulness. Our life is but a moment in time. Enjoy the moment. Chose joy.

April Words for 2017

1. Help others
2. Disciple
3. Care and compassion
4. Pray for patience
5. Faithful
6. Calm
7. Listen to wise counsel
8. Shine
9. Believe
10. Open heart
11. Choose faithfulness
12. Listen
13. God's will (best friend, Pat died today)
14. Consoling loving presence
15. Embrace one another
16. Love
17. The divine third
18. The glow of God's love
19. Encourage
20. An understanding heart
21. Breath of life/ breathe deeply
22. Joy
23. Divine Mercy
24. Try again
25. Speak with love
26. Shelter
27. Shine
28. Always a friend
29. Seek
30. Live in God's sunshine.

End of month reflections for April 2017

All of us go through difficult times in our lives. Since we understand how hard such times can be, we are called to help others.

"Bearing one another's burdens, and so you will fulfill the law of Christ" Gal. 6:2

To be Jesus' disciple, we are to take up whatever cross we bear and follow wherever God leads.

To show care and compassion is to understand the troubles of others. Continue to pray for patience in times of trials. Remain faithful and be a calm presence. Listen to wise counsel. Let the light of your faith shine. Believe and trust the open hearts of friends who show great love. Choose faithfulness to these friendships. Listen to your heart.

My dearest friend, Pat died today (April 13, 2017), God, in his great mercy willed to call her home. These are the times to be a consoling, loving presence. Time for embracing one another with hearts full of respect, peace, love, and understanding. Keep loving by acknowledging the divine third in friendships.

The glow of God's love will encourage everyone. All of us who have suffered a loss have developed an understanding heart. Breathe in deeply, the breath of life, realizing that in time we also will be called home to our maker.

There is unspeakable joy in life and in death. God's Divine Mercy gives us the grace to go on living our lives even though we have lost a loved one. We try again to be better at speaking with love. To be a shelter for each other. To let our lives be a shining example of God's love. To be a good friend. We seek God's will as we live in God's sunshine. Decide to be a light in any darkness.

I hear your silent cry.
I cry with you.
I feel your pain.
I hurt, too.
I sense your search for understanding.
I, also, long to know the reason, why?
I know you lift your heart in prayer.
I lift my heart as well.
It somehow meets and joins with yours.
We agree and are one with Him in love and compassion.
This is called friendship.
It is good.
God is the divine third in all life giving relationships.
Loving you…

Words for September 2013

1. Humble
2. Provided
3. Sheltered
4. Encourage
5. Purpose
6. Guide
7. Safe
8. Inspiration
9. Faithful
10. Friend
11. Together
12. Be thankful
13. Jesus
14. Trust
15. Lead and guide
16. Listen
17. All is well
18. Shelter
19. Joyful
20. Peace of Soul
21. Keep it simple
22. Praise
23. God's will
24. Faithful
25. Rest
26. Forever
27. Respect
28. Tender
29. Healing touch
30. Faith

End of month reflections for September 2013

Lord, I have been made humble and I am fearful. Yet, you have always provided for my well-being. I know I have been sheltered from more storms than I will ever know. Help me to encourage others who are uncertain about their life purpose.

Please guide me to a safe place of inspiration. Help me to always be a faithful friend and may we, together in union with your will, be thankful for the privilege of following Jesus. Help me to trust each of life's experiences by taking your lead and letting you guide me safely in love. Help me to listen for your call and to know that "all is well."

Thank you for the shelter you provide. Help me to have a joyful peace of soul. Peacefulness comes by keeping life simple and uncluttered and by slowing down.

Praise the Lord! Keep me in God's will. Help me to be a faithful witness. I come to you, Lord, for the rest I need. Help me to be forever faithful to your call. Help me to show respect to those in authority over me. I need your tender healing touch. Help me to keep and grow the blessings of faith.

Words for October 2013

1. Time
2. Angels
3. Encourage
4. Peace
5. Many blessings
6. Faithful
7. All is well
8. Keep it simple
9. Prayer
10. God's love
11. Bless the Lord
12. Walk with God
13. Love from the heart
14. Forgiveness
15. Listen for truth
16. Wait/be quiet
17. Be silent
18. Keep it simple
19. Listen well and speak less
20. Accept it
21. All is well
22. Goodness
23. Walk by faith
24. Joy
25. Hope
26. Trust in God's wisdom
27. Give
28. Prayer and work
29. Joy
30. Faith
31. Kindness

End of month reflections for October 2013

Life is just one moment in time. How we spend our time makes a difference. We all have angels who encourage us along our journey. If we but listen, peace and many blessings come out of our being faithful and loving. Whatever happens, we must let it unfold with trust and love, realizing that all is well.

Keep your life simple by not sinning. Sin will complicate your life. Sin will affect others. Your prayers are heard. God's love is always with you. "Bless the Lord, oh my soul."

Walk with God on your life's journey and love from the heart. Forgive those who have hurt you. Seek forgiveness for your sins.

In times of distress, pray and listen for truth, by waiting in silence. Keep it simple, listen well, and speak less. Accept what you cannot change, knowing again that all is well. The goodness in all hearts that walk by faith brings joy and hope to the world.

We must trust in God's wisdom and give glory to him. Life is about prayer and work done joyfully. We must keep our faith strong. By keeping our faith strong, we are able to show deep kindness to others.

Words for November 2013

1. Joy
2. Give
3. Yes, Lord
4. Jesus
5. Encourage
6. Listen with love
7. Goodness
8. Truth
9. Friendship
10. Shelter
11. Trust
12. Lead me
13. Thank you
14. Home
15. Trust in God
16. God's loving presence
17. Life
18. Grateful
19. Hope
20. Sheltered
21. Faith
22. Love
23. Shine
24. Blessings
25. Encourage
26. Silence
27. Praise you, Lord
28. Be a person of thankfulness
29. Goodness
30. Follow the law

End of month reflections for November 2013

It is a joy to serve the Lord, to give his love to others. Say yes to the Lord Jesus and to his call on your life. Encourage people; listen with a heart of love and goodness. The truth of good and holy friendships is that these help to shelter you in the storms that come in life.

Lord, I put my trust in you. Lead me on my life's journey. Thank you for the place I call home. I trust in God's loving presence in my life. I am grateful for the hope of a bright future for me and my loved ones. We are sheltered in a deep faith and God's love. It is God's Son shine and many blessings that give us strength and encouragement.

Even in the silence of our souls, we praise the Lord. We are a people of thankfulness. We seek goodness in all we do. We must follow the laws of the church and of the state. Do right! Do what is right!

Words for December 2013

1. Open
2. Faith
3. Journey
4. Protection
5. Truth
6. Give
7. Repent
8. Hope
9. Quiet
10. Encourage
11. Joy
12. Love
13. Blessings
14. Journeys
15. Kindness
16. Wonderful
17. Trust
18. God's presence
19. Goodness
20. Yes, Lord
21. Peace
22. Accept
23. Silence
24. Love
25. Hope
26. Something beautiful
27. Simple
28. Light
29. Balance
30. Worship
31. Jesus

End of month reflections for December 2013

Lord, open my heart to your truth and faithfulness on my journey toward heaven. Make me more aware of your protection. Give me the grace found in repentance and hope for the future.

Please quiet the fears that erupt. Encourage my soul with joy and love. Help me to see the many blessing on my daily journeys. Let kindness be forever in my heart. You, oh Lord, are wonderful and marvelous.

It is in God's loving presence and goodness that I place my trust. I give you my "yes, Lord" to the unknown, to faith. I accept the peace found in silence. The love of God and the hope that spring eternal creates something very beautiful in God's time.

Help me to keep my life simple. Let your light shine in my heart. Help me to keep a healthy balance everyday by worshiping God and making worship a key part of my daily schedule. Help me, Lord, to keep my heart focused on your goodness and on your great love for all of us.

I enjoy the Lord. I trust in his plans for my life's journey toward heaven. Jesus, help me to make right choices. Amen, amen.

(Remember: Every choice we make every day is a part of the sacred whole.)

2014

Words for January 2014

1. Commitment
2. Blessed
3. Respect
4. Truth
5. Treasures
6. Light
7. Love
8. Courage
9. Faith
10. Keep it simple
11. Journey
12. Do right
13. Trustworthy
14. Marvelous
15. Healing love
16. Thanks
17. Smile
18. Faith
19. Joy
20. Work
21. Be patient
22. Pray
23. God is in charge
24. Don't be afraid
25. Surrender
26. Compassion
27. Angels
28. Dance
29. All is well
30. Appreciate
31. Listen

End of month reflections for January 2014

We are blessed by the commitment, love, and respect of our family, friends, and co-workers. They see the truth of who we are. They are the treasures and light in our life that show us love. They give us the courage we need. Their faith strengthens our faith. They teach us to keep things simple and uncluttered on life's journey. They show by example to always do what is right. They are trustworthy and marvelous with their healing love.

We give thanks to God and to them. They make our heart smile. Our faith is a true joy. Our work is a great blessing. We just need to be more patient, pray, and give thanks for the jobs we have. We need to remember that God is in charge. We don't need to be afraid. We are in God's hands. All is well. Surrender every day, every moment to God.

Show compassion to others at all times. We have friends here and in high places. The angels dance around us, guarding, and protecting. All is well with our souls when we appreciate the special people who touch our lives. We should try to listen to what is needed and give ourselves as friend.

Words for February 2014

1. Treasures
2. Love
3. Faithfulness
4. God's healing love
5. Many blessings
6. Lead me
7. Light
8. Understanding heart
9. Be kind and generous
10. Hope
11. Wait
12. Be joyful
13. Faith of friends
14. Love
15. Inspiration
16. Respect
17. Compassion
18. Divine forces
19. Listen
20. Blessings
21. Faith
22. Shelters
23. Joy
24. Prayer and gentleness
25. Respect
26. If God wills
27. Change
28. Encourage

End of month reflections for February 2014

The greatest treasures in life are in the people that we let into our lives. It is through the love and faithfulness of family and friends that we experience God's healing love and many blessings.

God leads us in the right direction through the light of his love. He gives us an understanding heart. He opens our hearts to be kind and generous. Our hope is in God alone as we wait in prayer. Give God your love and devotion. He leads us to be joyful. He tells us to trust in him. Also, trust in the faith of family and friends. These people are an inspiration. Give them the respect and love that they deserve.

Know that Divine forces are standing guard. Listen for direction. As we honor that direction, many blessings will come our way. We are to have a great faith. Be aware of the shelters, the protection that surrounds us.

Live with a spirit of joy. Be a person of prayer. Show gentleness and respect to all the people in your life. Be mindful of the circumstance that, "If God wills" we may need to change. Be encouraged by the changes that happen. The reason will evolve and it will be good.

Words for March 2014

1. Childlike
2. Tender
3. Treasures
4. Simple
5. Openness to God's favor
6. Surrender
7. Joy smile
8. Great blessings
9. You are God's treasure
10. See the Good
11. Forgive
12. Simple
13. Beautiful
14. Truth
15. Children of God
16. Be a Blessing
17. Listen with your heart
18. Deep faith
19. Humble
20. Kindness
21. Wonderful plan
22. Psalm 121 Guardian
23. Listen to God
24. Peace
25. God blesses us
26. All is well
27. Sing praise
28. Love
29. Persevere
30. Listen
31. Keep on

End of month reflections words March 2014

Lord, create in us a childlike trust in you. Oh, Lord, in your mercy and tenderness are the treasures of a simple life. Create in us openness to your favor. We surrender our life to you with a joyful smile to the great blessings awaiting us.

We are God's greatest treasure when we see the good in each other and forgive. Strive to keep things simple and beautiful. Seek the truth as children of God. Be a blessing to others by listening to them with your whole heart. Pray for a deep abiding faith in God. Be humble in spirit, showing kindness and respect to all. God has a wonderful plan for our life. He is our guardian.

> *"I lift up my eyes toward the mountains; whence shall help come to me? My help is from the Lord, who made heaven and earth. May he not suffer your foot to slip; may he slumber not who guards you: Indeed he neither slumbers nor sleeps, the guardian of Israel. The Lord is your guardian; the Lord is your shade; he is beside you at your right hand. The sun shall not harm you by day, nor the moon by night. The Lord will guard you from all evil; he will guard your life. The Lord will guard your coming and your going, both now and forever"* (Ps. 121:1–8).

Listen to God in everything you do throughout each day. Be at peace knowing that God blesses us as we trust that all is well. Let us sing praise to God. His love endures forever. Persevere and listen to the leading of the Holy Spirit. Keep on keeping on.

Words for April 2014

Just "be" attitudes:

1. Be healing love
2. Be kind
3. Be quiet
4. Be faithful
5. Be a blessing
6. Be enlightened
7. Be calm
8. Be a faithful friend
9. Be light
10. Be loved
11. Be open
12. Be good
13. Be a person of prayer
14. Be gentle
15. Be a calming presence
16. Be thankful

17. Be joyful and be respectful
18. Be blameless
19. Be not afraid
20. Be risen (Easter) rise above your shortcomings
21. Just be
22. Be committed to what you do
23. Be present
24. Be spirit filled
25. Be patient
26. Be safe
27. Be at peace
28. Be yourself
29. Be fair
30. Be happy

Words for May 2014

1. Many blessings
2. Respect
3. Jesus
4. Home
5. Believe
6. Uncluttered
7. Joy
8. Listen
9. Do right
10. Calm
11. All is well
12. Safe
13. Trust
14. Blessings
15. Be kind
16. Dwelling place
17. God's presence
18. Jasper, Guardian angel
19. Treasure
20. Peace
21. Spiritual
22. Shelter
23. Simple
24. Grateful
25. Accept
26. Something beautiful
27. Respect
28. Spirit of the living God
29. Loving God, loving each other
30. Children of God
31. Goodness

End of month reflections for May 2014

Many blessings are coming your way, respect the blessings and give thanks. Let Jesus reign in your home. Believe and trust in the love you receive. Live an uncluttered life. Be a person of joy by listening to your heart and doing what is right.

Keep a calm disposition because all is well. Keep safe by trusting your instincts. Many blessings come from being kindhearted. Enjoy your home, your dwelling place. God's goodness and faithfulness to you is abundant. Your guardian angel protects and guides you. Give your guardian angel a name. (My guardian angel's name is Jasper.)

"For he will put his angels in charge over you to guard you in all your ways" (Ps. 91:11).

Treasure the peace in your heart. Peace is a spiritual shelter. Keep your life simple. Be grateful and accept the love given. No matter what you may be going through at the moment, God makes everything beautiful in his time. Have a deep respect for people. Share the spirit of the living God by loving God and loving each other. We are all children of God. There is great goodness in us.

Words for June 2014

1. God's presence
2. Yes, Lord
3. God
4. Patience
5. God loves me (happy birthday)
6. God is faithful
7. Follow Jesus
8. Come Holy Spirit
9. Encourage
10. Blessings
11. Many blessings
12. Shelter
13. Listen
14. Guidance
15. The gift of faith
16. Respect
17. Shine
18. Love
19. Father
20. Treasures
21. Trust
22. Nothing can separate
23. Rest in God's presence
24. Security
25. Simple
26. Friends
27. Be kind
28. In my heart
29. Joy
30. Listen

End of month reflections for June 2014

Seek God's presence in all you do. Say, Yes, Lord, to God's call on your life. Have patience with others.

(I know God loves me, he created me. Happy sixty-fourth birthday, Linda!)

God is faithful. We must be faithful in following Jesus. We ask, come Holy Spirit come. Be an encourager. We need to ask for blessings, many blessings. We ask you to shelter us, Lord, from the storms as we listen for your gentle guidance. Thank you, Lord, for the gift of faith. We respect the light that shines on us from the love of our heavenly Father.

Many treasures await us as we trust in God's goodness. We know that nothing can separate us from the love of God. We must take time to rest in God's presence. We have security in the simple joys of life. Friends are a great blessing. Be kind to your friends. They love you. Keep them close to your heart as they bring joy to your life. Listen to your heart. Do what is right. Take time to listen to the grass grow, listen to the snow fall.

Words for July 2014

1. Love and laugh
2. Seek the good
3. Trust
4. Blessings
5. Kindness and love
6. Peace in rest
7. Joy
8. Peaceful
9. God's presence
10. Expect the best
11. Simple
12. Faith
13. Goodness
14. Protected
15. Secure
16. Peaceful
17. Rest
18. Be blessed
19. Marvelous
20. Yield to the Spirit
21. Praise the Lord
22. Miracles
23. Faithful
24. Peace
25. Open heart
26. God's gift
27. Treasure
28. Shield
29. Truth
30. Encourage
31. Something beautiful

End of month reflections for July 2014

Since life is a journey, make sure you love and laugh along the way. Seek the good and trust your instincts. Expect many blessings of kindness and love each day. You will find restful peace as you joy in the peaceful presence of God.

You can expect the best blessings by keeping your life simple and uncluttered. Cherish your faith in the goodness of those you journey with each day. Know that you are in God's loving care. You are protected and secure in his love.

The peaceful rest of being blessed is a marvelous gift when you yield to the Holy Spirit's guidance and sing praise to the Lord. Miracles are unfolding as you remain faithful to the God of peace.

Open your heart to God's many gifts. Treasure your family, friends, neighbors and co-workers. Prayerfully shield them from what is not the truth. Let us encourage each other along the way of making something beautiful of our lives. Be a blessing to all.

Words for August 2014

1. Silence
2. Make Godly choices
3. Gifts
4. Hope
5. Healing
6. Listen to Jesus
7. All is well
8. Divine Supply
9. Faith
10. Such a blessing
11. God is in charge
12. Guide
13. Shelter
14. Pay it forward
15. Faithful
16. Rest
17. Sunshine
18. Treasure
19. Humble
20. I place my life in your loving hands
21. Humble
22. Encourage
23. Resting Place
24. God's gifts
25. Open Heart
26. Treasure
27. Quiet
28. Angels
29. Jesus
30. Gifts
31. Support

End of month reflections for August 2014

It is best to seek the silence of the heart and soul when deciding to make godly choices in life. The gifts of the Holy Spirit lead to hope. Healing evolves when we listen to Jesus. We also come to realize that all is well. Divine supply for our faith is such a blessing. God is in charge. He will guide and shelter us.

Pay it forward by living and being witness to a faithful service of love. To do this well, we must take time for the rest we need. Get a little sunshine in our day. Treasure the moments of encounter with others. Be a humble, loving presence. Place your life in God's loving hands.

Dear Lord, thou art worthy. We humble ourselves before you. Thank you for encouraging us to that resting place. Thank you for the many gifts you have prepared for our open hearts. We treasure the quiet times. We realize the protection of your holy angels. Thank you for the gift of your loving son, Jesus, our treasured redeemer and support.

Words for September 2014

1. Day of rest from our Labor
2. Spirit of God
3. Sheltered in the loving arms
4. Seeing God's love
5. Peaceful
6. Showers of blessings
7. Safe place
8. Walk in God's love
9. Do right
10. Be joyful
11. Open Heart
12. One moment in Time
13. Enjoy the gift of quiet
14. Faith
15. Mary, Mother of God
16. Tenderness
17. God's love
18. Goodness
19. Joy
20. In God we trust
21. Home
22. Blessings
23. Wonderful
24. All is well
25. God is in Control
26. Honor
27. Journey toward our heavenly home
28. Peaceful
29. Do what is right
30. Enjoy the journey

End of month reflections for September 2014

Do your best to take a day of rest from your labor. Let the Spirit of God shelter you in His loving arms. Keep your heart open to seeing God's love through each other. Have a peaceful soul. Shower blessings by being a safe place for each other as we walk together in God's love.

Do what is right and just. Be a joyful presence. Keep your heart open to each special moment in time. Enjoy the gifts that come from a quiet restful spirit. This helps to keep your faith strong.

Allow Mary, the Mother of God, to be your guide in showing tenderness and the goodness of God's love. Smile and keep the joy of God's Holy Spirit alive in your heart. Remember, it is "In God we trust."

Let your home be a blessing to all who visit, so each person will feel wonderful for stopping by. Let others know that all is well. God is truly in control. Show respect and honor to all as you journey toward your Heavenly home.

By being a peaceful presence, you help others to do what is right. Keep praising the Lord and enjoying the journey with God in your heart.

Words for October 2014

1. Prosperity
2. Guardian angels
3. Be at peace
4. Light
5. Forever Friend
6. Lord, what would you do?
7. Many blessings
8. Be faithful
9. Encourage
10. Service with a smile
11. Listen
12. Endurance
13. Praise the Lord
14. Be kind
15. Goodness
16. Simple
17. Safe
18. Love with God
19. Forever friend
20. Treasure
21. Listen
22. Be open
23. God has placed you where you are
24. Lord, Help me
25. God makes everything beautiful

26. Open Heart   28. Respect   30. Wait on God
27. Be kind hearted   29. Do right   31. Persevere

End of month reflections for October 2014

Lord, thank you for the gift of prosperity. Help us to be wise and generous in our giving. Thank you for the protection of our guardian angels. We are at peace when we let your light shine in our life. Thank you for all the forever friends, the saints you placed in our life's journey that shows us what you would do. Thank you for the many blessings of having faithful friends. Thank you for their encouragement and their service with a smile.

Help us to listen to the guidance of the Holy Spirit, to endure with courage and joy in our daily task. We praise you, Lord, for the kindness you always show. We pray that the goodness of a simple, safe, life with the love of God in our whole being will shine as a forever friend that others will treasure.

Help us to listen and be open to the interruptions that come to us throughout the day, to count them as blessings from you. Help us to understand that you have placed us where we are for a good reason. Lord, help us to do right.

We know that you make everything beautiful in your time. We open our hearts to you so that we can be more kindhearted and respectful. Sometimes to do what is right requires waiting on God and it requires perseverance.

Words for November 2014

1. Shelter   6. Humble   11. Perseverance
2. Goodness   7. Blessings   12. Kindness
3. Faith   8. Gifts   13. Wait
4. Simple   9. Let your light shine 14. Positive
5. Trust   10. Forgive   15. Contentment

16. Model of faith
17. Quiet peaceful life
18. Service for the Lord
19. Seek the Lord
20. Life giving choices
21. God is Love
22. Be at Peace
23. Lead me
24. Do your work with joy
25. Responsibility
26. Amen
27. Make a difference
28. Blessings
29. Goodness
30. Seek the Lord

End of month reflections for November 2014

God, our Father, thank you for the shelter and the goodness that our faith creates. Our simple trust and humble witness brings many blessings. Our family is a gift from you. We are a gift to them. They help us to let our light shine as they forgive us when we fail.

Lord, help us to persevere in kindness and to wait for your guidance. Help us to have a positive outlook. Help us to be content as things unfold according to your will. Help us to wait in prayer and to be at peace knowing that you will work everything out for our good. Lord, help us to be models of great faith in our quiet peaceful lives of service to you.

We seek your will as we make life giving choices. We know, Lord, that you are love. We are at peace because all is well in your presence. Help us to do our work with joy in our hearts.

We accept our responsibility to always do what is right. Amen, Lord, Amen and thank you for the difference you make in our lives. We accept the many blessings you give us. Surely goodness and your mercy will be ours as we seek the Lord and his will.

Words for December 2014

1. Healing
2. Friend
3. Kindness
4. Peace
5. Light
6. Quiet
7. Strength
8. Hope
9. Honor
10. Security
11. Miracles

12. Mary, Mother of God
13. Miracles
14. Wonderful
15. Journey
16. Joy
17. Blessings
18. Angels
19. Listen
20. Believe
21. Surrender
22. God's goodness
23. Embrace God's plan
24. Trust in God
25. Listen
26. Faithfulness
27. Friendship
28. God's love
29. Encourage
30. Do good
31. Jesus

End of month reflections for December 2014

God's healing love is the true friend in kindnesses shown. His healing love brings peace and lights our way. His healing love gives us a quiet strength and hope for the future. We honor the security found in God's healing love, as many miracles unfold. The loving Mary, Mother of God, prays for us as more miracles flow into our paths. How wonderful our life's journey can be as we joyfully anticipate and accept the blessings of each day.

We join our voices with the angels in singing praise to our creator. We listen carefully with our hearts to those around us. We believe and surrender our lives to God's goodness. We embrace God's plan and place our trust in Him.

As we listen with our heart and acknowledge His faithfulness, all of our friendships are filled with God's love. These friendships encourage us to keep doing what is right and good in Jesus's loving presence.

2015

Words for January 2015

1. Guide
2. Love
3. Wait on the Lord
4. All is well
5. Healing presence
6. Miracle
7. Trust in God
8. Hope
9. Be calm
10. Joy in God's presence
11. God is with us
12. Listen
13. Adventure
14. Be present
15. Be faithful
16. Friend
17. Silence
18. Faith
19. Receive
20. All is well
21. Believe
22. Shelter
23. Quiet and gentle spirit
24. Sing praise to God
25. Safe
26. Blessings
27. Be patient
28. Goodness
29. All is well
30. Choose good thoughts
31. Shelter

End of month reflections for January 2015

God will guide us and show us the way of abiding love. When in doubt, prayerfully wait on God to renew your strength. Know in your heart that all is well in the healing presence of love. Miracles happen when we trust God. There is always hope for the future.

We can remain calm during troubled times as we find joy in God's loving presence in our life. Yes, God is with us. God is on our side. Listen to the promptings of the Holy Spirit. Each day is an adventure planned by God. Be aware of God's presence and be present to others (be there for them). Be a faithful friend. Silence is better than misspoken words.

Keep your faith strong. Receive the gifts of love, believing that all is well. You are sheltered in God's loving embrace. Go forth with a quiet and gentle spirit toward all. Sing praise to God for the safety he provides. Graciously receive the blessings that enter your days. Be very patient and show goodness to all. Remember again and again that all is well.

Choose good thoughts each day. These good thoughts will provide shelter from the storms of life and hope for the sunshine.

Words for February 2015

1. Walk by faith
2. Seek the face of God
3. Trust God
4. Accept yourself
5. Peace
6. Respect
7. Rest in God
8. Balance
9. Goodness
10. Loving presence
11. Wait
12. Positive
13. Treasures
14. Love
15. Right attitude
16. Quiet peace
17. Save
18. Be thankful
19. Angels
20. Trust
21. Healing Love
22. Share
23. Be thankful
24. Endure
25. Silence
26. Friendship
27. Endure with love and laughter
28. Blessing

End of month reflections for February 2015

God calls us to walk by faith on our life's journey. To help us along this path, we seek the face of God. We learn to trust in God's goodness when we accept ourselves and our circumstances. We do our best when we let God's peace shine in our lives.

We gain peace of soul as we learn to respect our times of resting and trusting in God's presence. We can find balance in our lives by realizing God's goodness and knowing that God's loving presence is always available to us—Just accept this truth.

Our attitudes become more positive as we learn from the treasures of his love and his goodness. It is of great importance to get the right attitude on our life's journey. Even in troubled times, we can have a quiet peace in our hearts.

It is God who saves us. We are to be thankful people who endure to the end with a lot of love and hearty laughter. We are given many blessings on our journey. A host of angels are among us as we trust all to God. His healing love is to be shared with a thankful heart. We can endure to the end because God's love endures.

Silence is better than inappropriate words used to hurt. Be true to the friendships that have been gifted to you. These friendships matter and help make you a better person. Be thankful for the marvelous and wonderful gifts of friendships. These are the people who make our hearts smile. Be that kind of friend to others.

Words for March 2015

1. Shower love
2. Wonderful
3. Be gentle
4. Blessings
5. Trust God
6. Hope
7. Guide
8. God's great love
9. Faith
10. Kindness
11. Laugh more
12. Obedience
13. Peace
14. Persevere
15. Prayer
16. Believe
17. Be calm
18. Listen carefully
19. Angels
20. Wait
21. Be open to God's presence
22. All is well
23. Forgive
24. Security
25. Goodness
26. A humble heart
27. Be joyful
28. Shelter
29. Persevere
30. Wait
31. Shine

End of month reflections for March 2015

Into everyone's life showers will fall. Wonderful showers of love. Accept these showers as gentle blessings from a trustful God to give us hope and to guide us. God's great love expands our faith and opens our heart to the kindness of others. Showers of forgiveness can help wash away our sins and free us to enjoy life more and to laugh again. To keep this joy, we must be obedient to God's laws and love. It is his peace in us that will help us persevere through all of life's trials. Prayer is the key to all of life.

Believe in God and be calm in his presence. Listen carefully to the promptings of the Holy Spirit. God's angels are always available. They wait—standing guard to protect. Be open to God's presence in all of life. Know in your heart that all is well.

Forgive yourself when you fail. Keep doing what is right. You are secure in the palm of God's hands. Be joyful, knowing you are sheltered in the midst of life's storms. Persevere through the storms and wait in God's love. The sun will shine again. Blessings and sunshine!

Words for April 2015

1. Simple
2. Humble
3. Purpose
4. Wait
5. Rise/Shine
6. Encourage
7. God
8. Healing love
9. Do right
10. Obey
11. Do not complain
12. Peace
13. Be gentle
14. Marvelous
15. Keep calm
16. Love
17. Abundance
18. Do not be afraid
19. Everlasting love
20. Believe
21. Live life
22. Work
23. Guidance
24. Shelter
25. Kindness
26. Rest
27. Open Heart
28. Faithful
29. The kindness of a blessing
30. All is well

End of month reflections words April 2015

How do you keep your life simple? Try taking one day at a time. Be humble in dealing with others. They also have a purpose. When you don't know what to do, wait in prayer before God. God will direct your path. You will confidently rise and shine with the encouragement and strength of God's healing love. The simple solution is to always do right and obey the commands of God.

Do not complain (about anything)! You can have peace of soul by being a gentle spirit. It is truly a marvelous experience when you keep calm and show love. The abundance of love will grow. Do not be afraid. God's love is an everlasting love. Believe! Live your life. Work daily in God's presence. Being aware of God's guidance and the shelter of his protection leads you to a greater kindness with those you encounter.

When you get distracted, take a moment to rest in his presence with an open heart. God is faithful. You be faithful, too. Accept the kindness of his blessings. Be a blessing to others. Know in your heart that all is well. God is love.

Words for May 2015

1. Knowing God
2. Jesus
3. Marvelous
4. Healing love
5. Blessings
6. Simple
7. Trust
8. Listen
9. Respect
10. Be thankful
11. Patient endurance
12. Treasure
13. Do right
14. Believe
15. Holy Spirit
16. Today
17. Abundance
18. Hope
19. Secure
20. Faithful
21. Persistent
22. Friendship
23. Focus on your blessings
24. Abundance
25. Shelter
26. Change
27. Patience
28. Breathe
29. Be thankful
30. Joyful heart
31. Believe

End of month reflections words May 2015

Knowing God, the Father, Jesus, the Son, and the Holy Spirit creates a marvelous healing love through the blessings of a simple trusting faith. Listen to the voice of wisdom and show respect. Be thankful to God for his patient endurance when we fail to treasure the gift of faith. Do what is right by believing and trusting in the guidance of the Holy Spirit.

God is the abundance of love. We do have hope and a secure tomorrow. We must remain faithful followers and have a persistent friendship with the Holy Trinity. By focusing on our many blessings, we realize the life of abundance we live under the shelter of Almighty God.

When changes come with the cycles of life, we patiently breathe in deeply and smile as we let out the breath called life. We know we are going to our new heavenly home. It is with a joyful, thankful heart that we accepted the gift of faith, the belief in the Father, the Son, and the Holy Spirit.

A lifelong journey: Wherever you are, be all there and be thankful.

Words for June 2015

1. Remain calm
2. Trust in God
3. Live well
4. Praise the Lord
5. Protected by angels
6. Seek the Lord
7. Jesus
8. Faith
9. Let you light shine
10. God's presence
11. God's peace
12. Blessings
13. Trust
14. Lead and Guide
15. Encourage one another
16. Be calm
17. Jesus
18. Wait
19. Treasure
20. Believe
21. Joy
22. Be thankful
23. Guide me
24. Listen intently
25. Friendship
26. Stay calm
27. Kindness
28. God's presence
29. Give it all to Jesus
30. Sunshine

End of month reflections for June 2015

Our lives will have many challenges. We need to remind ourselves to breathe deeply and remain calm by trusting in God's loving presence. We do our best by living well and praising God in all situations. He sends his angels to protect and guide us. We should always seek the Lord, Jesus. He loves us and helps us to keep our faith strong so we can be a light that shines for all to witness God's presence in our life.

When we have God's peace, our lives are a blessing to others. Trust and obey the promptings of the Holy Spirit to lead and guide. Encourage one another and be a calm presence. See Jesus in each relationship. Wait in silence and treasure the love that others have for us. Believe in the goodness of others. What a joy it is to be around people who are thankful. Guide us, Lord, so we will listen intently to what is being said.

Let friendships grow by staying calm and showing loving kindness. God's presence is in each friendship. Give your troubles to Jesus. He will give you strength, courage, and hope. Live in the light of Sunshine. Spend time in the light of God's love.

Words for July 2015

1. Love and laugh
2. Happy heart
3. Roses
4. Keep life simple
5. Thankful heart
6. Persevere
7. Faithful
8. God's will
9. Listen
10. Choose rightly
11. Seek God
12. Jesus
13. Expect the best
14. Protected
15. Trust
16. Safe place
17. Surrender
18. Faith
19. Marvelous
20. Simple
21. Be thankful
22. Do right
23. Light
24. Protect
25. Wonderful
26. Hope
27. Take the high road
28. Transforming presence
29. Lighten up
30. Life journey
31. Thankful

End of month reflections words July 2015

Live your life with heartfelt love and laughter, keeping a happy heart by taking time to "smell the roses." The best way to do this is to keep your life simple. Have a thankful heart. Persevere through hard times by faithfully following God's will.

Listen carefully to what his word says. You can choose rightly when you seek God. Look to Jesus and expect the best. You are protected. Simply do the best you can. Trust God to keep you in a safe place.

When you surrender all to him in faith, marvelous experiences unfold before you. It is simple. You must be a thankful person and do right by everyone.

Let God's light shine through you. Protect your relationships with wonderful love. Keep hope alive by always taking the high road. The transforming presence of God helps to lighten up your life's journey. Always have a thankful heart.

Words for August 2015

1. God's Blessings
2. Enjoy the Lord
3. Moments
4. Secure
5. Be quiet
6. Responsibility
7. All is well
8. Thankful heart
9. Commitment
10. God's transforming love
11. Be kind
12. Responsible
13. Relax
14. Journey of faith
15. Seek the Lord
16. Rest
17. Sunshine
18. Be nice
19. Wait
20. Healing
21. Joy
22. Trust
23. Follow Jesus
24. Friend
25. Tender
26. Inner calm
27. Companion
28. Serve
29. What's important?
30. Change
31. Take God's hand

End of month reflections words August 2015

God's many blessings send us out into the world each day to enjoy his presence in each moment of our life. We are secure in his love. Take time to be quiet in his presence before you take on the responsibilities of the day. This way you can have a fresh start, knowing that all is well before him.

With a thankful heart, renew your commitment of accepting God's healing and transforming love. Be kind to the people you encounter today. Be a responsible, trustworthy soul. Take the time during a hectic day to relax and remind yourself that you are on a journey of faith and must continue to seek the Lord by resting in his presence. Spend some time in his sunshine and feel his love.

Be a nice, caring person to those who are hurting. Wait in silence before you speak. God's healing will bring you joy as you trust the Holy Spirit and follow Jesus. Jesus is your friend and your tender companion that gives you the inner calm you need to serve him. Realize what is important and what really matters. He changes your outlook and your attitude. Take God's hand and follow where he leads.

Our days have meaning and purpose that endure beyond this day and this place.

Words for September 2015

1. Be supportive
2. Listen to God
3. Be at peace
4. Heart of Jesus
5. Let God help
6. Open heart
7. Prayer and work
8. Expect the best
9. Trust in the Lord
10. Breath
11. Rejoice
12. Quietness
13. Jesus
14. Love
15. Persevere
16. Transform
17. Peace
18. Shelter
19. Listen carefully
20. Trust in God

21. Lay it all before the Lord	24. Goodness	28. Hope
22. Strength	25. Work for God	29. Angels
23. Light	26. Serve	30. Wisdom
	27. Remember	

End of month reflections for September 20015

    We can learn to be more supportive of each other when we listen to God's word. We can be at peace when we stay close to the heart of Jesus. We let God help us when we keep our hearts open and prayerfully do our work. We can expect the best when we put our trust in the Lord. He is our breath of life. We rejoice in the goodness of the Lord.

    In the quietness of our soul, we allow Jesus's love to help us persevere through our trials. He transforms our life. We find peace as we rest in the shelter of his presence. Listen very carefully to what we hear in the silence of our soul. Trust in God as we lay all our cares before him. He is our strength and our light. Surely his goodness and mercy will follow us in our work done for God. He is with us. We serve him well in all we do. Our work is to honor him. Hope always in the Lord, who made heaven and earth. His angels are watching over us. Seek his wisdom and follow him.

    Invest in the future: Spending time with God is a wise investment!

Words for October 2015

1. Treasure each day	6. Walk in the light	11. Moments
2. Guardian	7. Mercy	12. Helpful
3. Trust in God	8. All is well	13. Be faithful
4. Friends	9. Joy	14. Give thanks
5. Yes, Lord and help me	10. God's abundant supply	15. Holy Spirit
		16. Blessings

17. Be a witness to the faith
18. Trust and obey
19. Free
20. Abundant
21. God will provide
22. Kindness
23. God's peace
24. Holy Spirit
25. Jesus
26. Be better
27. Home
28. Presence
29. Depend on God
30. Truth
31. Walk

End of month reflections for October 2015

Learn to treasure each day as a beautiful gift. Let God be the guardian of your soul. His angels encircle you in safety. "Jasper, my guardian angel, protects me from myself." Always trust in God and the fellowship of friends. Say yes to the Lord and seek his help by walking in his light. Let God's mercy enfold you.

Sometimes it is up to us to allow all to be well. Attain a spirit of joy in God's abundant supply. Treasure moments of opportunities to be helpful and faithful always giving thanks to God who sustains us.

Be led by the Holy Spirit. Many blessings flow by being a witness to the faith. Always trust and obey. Live free of addictions to have an abundant life. God will provide. Let kindness and mercy guide your works and God's peace will be received in full measure.

Let the Holy Spirit and Jesus be your guide to being a better person. Be at home with who you are in God's presence. You can depend on God. Accept truth and walk humbly with your God.

Mercy: more kindness than justice requires. Kindness beyond what can be claimed or expected.

Words for November 2015

1. Change
2. Give
3. Forgive
4. Peace
5. Free
6. Goodness
7. Blessings
8. Child of God
9. Friendship
10. All is well
11. Wonderful
12. Abundance

13. The love of God
14. Father, Son, and Holy Spirit
15. Trust
16. Serve
17. Simple
18. Joyful giving
19. Love
20. Simple
21. Live
22. Shelter
23. Love and Goodness
24. Keep your eyes on Jesus
25. Pray
26. Blessings
27. Endearing
28. Believe
29. Seeking
30. Peace

End of month reflections for November 2015

Our circumstances in life will change. Whatever happens, we must trust God and give our life journey over to him. Learn to forgive others and forgive ourselves so we can be at peace and be free. Allow all the goodness and blessings as a child of God and the friendship of all the saints to flow into our life, knowing that all is well.

Keep on loving. God is so wonderful. He has an overwhelming abundance of love through the trinity: The Father, the Son, and the Holy Spirit. Trust in God and serve him well. Keep your life simple. Be a joyful giver. Keep love simple by living life well.

We are sheltered in God's love and goodness. We will know this by keeping our eyes on Jesus and by praying for guidance. God's many blessings, enduring love, and faithfulness are available for those who believe. Keep seeking to know God and his peace.

Words for December 2015

1. Responsible
2. Mercy
3. Journey
4. Marvelous
5. Give
6. Repent
7. Walk with joy
8. Beautiful
9. Hope
10. God is in control
11. Expect great things
12. Jesus
13. Smile more, be joyful
14. Respect
15. Trust
16. Faithfulness

17. Praise the Lord
18. Do right
19. God's presence
20. Amazing
21. Believe
22. Peaceful heart
23. Light
24. God's peace
25. Simple
26. Relax
27. Light
28. Friendship
29. Trust in God
30. Journey together
31. Jesus

End of month reflections for December 2015

We are responsible for our own actions, no one else. Through God's mercy, we are forgiven of our sins. We do have to seek forgiveness and strive to live better. Our life's journey can be marvelous if we marvel at the wonderfulness of being able to talk and walk with God each day. Give God the benefit of any doubts we may have. We need to repent of our sins, so we can walk with joy and have beautiful hope for our future. Let God be in control and expect great things. When we allow Jesus to be our guide, we become more loving.

Smile more and be a joyful person. Respect where others are on their Christian journey. Trust in their process and their faithfulness. Praise the Lord along our journey. Always do what is right. Be aware of God's presence. His amazing presence. When we believe in God's love, we will have a peaceful heart. The light of Jesus guides us to God's peace. Keep our life simple by relaxing and not trying to solve other people's problems. Their problems have a purpose. Let them handle what they have created. Be forever true to your friendships. Trust God as we journey together. Always allow Jesus to be the divine third in every relationship.

2016

Words for January 2016

1. Change
2. Seek
3. Choose right
4. Blessed
5. Faith
6. Guide me
7. Wonderful
8. Be calm
9. Path to goodness
10. Trust
11. Listen
12. Jesus
13. Friends
14. Marvelous
15. Relax
16. Humble
17. Silence
18. Be a blessing
19. Surrender
20. Restful
21. Healing
22. Faithfulness
23. Gentle and quiet spirit
24. Faith
25. Surrender
26. Keep calm
27. Tenderness
28. Walk in faith
29. Quietly and gently
30. Openness
31. Love

End of month reflections for January 2016

     Be ready to accept change because change is always on the horizon. We must continue to seek the Lord and to choose the right course. Choose Jesus every day. Your life is a blessed life. Your faith will guide you. Faith is a wonderful gift, treasure your faith. Be calm, choose the path of goodness. Trust the Holy Spirit's guidance. Listen to Jesus's words found in the Bible. Write God's words on your heart. Choose your friends wisely. Seek wise counsel.

Life will be difficult at times but let it be a marvelous journey. Take time to relax in God's presence. Humble yourself before the Lord. Set in silence with him. Let your life be a blessing. Surrender everything to his love. His healing will flow through you.

When words fail, be a gentle, quiet, spiritual presence. In faith surrender everything to God. He makes everything beautiful in his time. He can keep you calm through the storms. His tenderness is always there for you. Walk with God quietly, gently in faith. Seek restful time alone with God and have openness to all his love.

Words for February 2016

1. Discernment
2. Reconciliation
3. Believe
4. Weakness
5. God has the solution
6. Listening heart
7. Miracle
8. God is in control
9. Life is a journey
10. Peace
11. Heed
12. Faithfulness
13. Abundance
14. Joy
15. Inspiration
16. Hear and respond
17. Hold tight
18. Transformed
19. Endure
20. Thankfulness
21. Kindness
22. Endurance
23. Walk by faith
24. Jesus saves
25. Prayerfully wait
26. Forgive
27. Peace
28. Healing

End of month reflections for February 2016

How do we define the best course of action for our circumstances? Discernment, seek keenness in seeing and understanding God's will. Use good judgment. Go to God in prayer for reconciliation, the act of bringing together again in friendship.

Believe in God to help you overcome your weaknesses. God has the solution to your problems. Develop a listening heart and believe that miracles do happen when we surrender to God. Let him have control.

Life is a journey. We must let Christ walk with us. God's peace flows when we heed his voice. In faithfulness, we accept the abundance of his love and allow joy to return to our spirit. We receive inspiration when we hear and respond to his call to hold tight and hang on to his hand.

We are transformed by his love and able to endure through the storms. The peace of Christ calms our heart. With a heart full of thankfulness and loving kindness, we are able to endure our trials (not through self-pity.)

We continue to walk by faith with Jesus who saves us from evil. Prayerfully wait on God to work his miracles. We must forgive others, so we can live in peace and continue our quest for healing.

Words for March 2016

1. Forgive
2. Divine
3. Purity
4. Guide me
5. Shelter
6. Love and laugh
7. God's favor
8. Hope
9. The love of Christ
10. Humble
11. Faith
12. Simple
13. Peace
14. Persevere
15. Gifts
16. Truth
17. Calm
18. Listen
19. Stay
20. Thankful heart
21. All is well
22. Patience
23. Abundance
24. Faithful
25. Forgive
26. Wait on the Lord
27. Believe for God's best
28. Walk with God
29. Simple
30. Listen
31. Persevere

End of month reflections for March 2016

A Prayer

Lord, forgive me of my sins. In your divine mercy, have pity on me. Help me to always seek the divine connections you provide to guide me in the way of purity. Guide me to the shelter of your loving embrace.

Teach me to love and laugh in your divine favor that last for a lifetime. I have hope in the love of Christ. I am humbled and ask for a great faith as I keep my life simple. Help me to not back out of my commitments, to always follow through. Give me peace as I persevere through troubled times. Thank you for the many gifts of truth, love, and friendships. You give me a calm heart as I listen to you through your word and the gifts of the Holy Spirit.

Help me to stay focused with a thankful heart and trust in you that all is well. Give me the gift of patience when dealing with others. Help me to be a faithful person, to forgive as I prayerfully wait on your guidance before I respond.

I believe in your best plan for me as I walk with you. I know that keeping life simple by listening to you, the guidance of the Holy Spirit, and the protection of the angels; I can persevere through all life challenges.

Words for April 2016

1. Jesus
2. Presence
3. Divine Mercy
4. Treat people with dignity
5. Quietness
6. Blessings
7. Expect the best
8. Change
9. Encourage
10. Believe
11. Love
12. Faithfulness
13. Be gentle
14. Marvelous
15. Keep calm
16. Give Thanks
17. Listen to God
18. Wait
19. Have a blessed day
20. Be still
21. God's grace

22. Listen to the Lord
23. Rest in Christ
24. Be still
25. God bless
26. Hope
27. Abundant
28. Trust in God's mercy
29. God's plan
30. Wait on the Lord

End of month reflections for April 2016

It is through acknowledging Jesus's presence and his divine mercy in our lives that we will be able to treat others with respect and dignity. It is through the quietness of time spent pondering God's will for our life that helps create the flow of many blessings.

We can expect the best out of each change that will come into our life. Encourage each other to believe and to love the faithfulness of God. Be a gentle spirit through the marvelous love of God. Keep a calm disposition. Give thanks in all circumstances.

Listen to God and wait for his guidance through the Holy Spirit. You can have a blessed day when you take time to be still in God's grace, to listen to the Lord by way of the Holy Spirit.

Love and joy flow through resting and being still in Christ presence. God's blessings will flow through and give hope for the future. God's abundant blessings are already in your life, count your blessings. (Right now, count your blessings!)

Trust in God's mercy and trust in God's plan for your life. Wait on the Lord to lead you. Seek his presence.

Words for May 2016

1. Child of God
2. Holy Spirit
3. Be joyful
4. Believe
5. Hope
6. Security
7. God's Blessings
8. Rest and keep life simple
9. God's gifts
10. Open heart
11. Trusting
12. All is Well
13. Accept God's Grace
14. Goodness
15. Tender
16. Uncluttered

17. Stability	21. Father, Son, and Holy Spirit	25. Peacemaker
18. God willing	22. Help others	26. Discipline
19. Positive influences	23. Shower many blessings	27. Commitment
20. Choose to believe	24. Deliver	28. Gifts
		29. God is Good
		30. God's peace

End of month reflections for May 2016

Since you are a child of God, trust and believe that all is well. Let the Holy Spirit guide you to be joyful as you believe in the hope and security of God's many blessings. Rest in God's tender, loving arms. Keep your life simple.

As an excited child, receive God's gifts with an open heart always trusting that all is well. Simply accept God's grace and rest in his goodness. Have a tender love for others. Keep your life uncluttered.

When things seem to be going wrong, look at the true stability in your life by counting your blessings. God is always willing and able to help you. Just seek Him. Look to the people in your life that are positive influences and persevere in loving. Choose to believe and trust in the Father, Son, and the Holy Spirit.

As you help others, you receive showers of blessings. Hold to God's hand. He will deliver you. Be a peacemaker and have discipline in your commitments. Let the gifts of the Holy Spirit guide you. God is good—yes, good all the time. Accept God's peace.

Words for June 2016

1. Faithfully	5. Angels guard	10. Silence
2. Transforming power	6. Choose peace	11. Balance
3. Praise God	7. Believe	12. Wisdom
4. Lead me	8. Respect	13. Love is love
	9. Joyful love	14. Hope

15. Shelter
16. Simple
17. Jesus
18. Wait
19. Follow the path of obedience
20. Believe, wall of protection
21. Be still
22. Be thankful
23. Beautiful
24. God's plan
25. Be watchful
26. Hope
27. Sheltered/ praise God
28. Joy
29. Lead me/ guide me
30. Balance

End of month reflections for June 2016

Faithfully believe and trust in the transforming power of God's love. Praise God as he continuously leads and guides you. His angels guard you. Be at peace by choosing peace. Believe in and respect the joyful love you give and receive.

In the silence of your heart, seek the balance and wisdom you need in your life. Remember that love is love (God is love.) Hope in the future. God's shelter is always found in simple trust. Let Jesus's example of waiting in prayer and then following the path of obedience and mercy lead you to God's will.

Believe in the wall of protection around you. Don't rush to judgments. Be still and be a thankful person. God is creating something very beautiful in your life. God has a plan so be watchful. You have hope for the future. You are sheltered in God's loving embrace. Praise God! There is joy in life as you let God lead and guide you. Live a balanced life.

Words for July 2016

1. Be kind
2. Faith
3. Loving heart
4. Simple
5. Praise God
6. Listen to Godly counsel
7. Do right
8. Be loyal
9. Respect for others
10. Miracles
11. Do good
12. Trust and be not afraid

13. Be helpful and expect good	18. Walk humbly	26. Compassion
	19. Speak gently	27. Hope
14. Rest in God's peace	20. Simple	28. God's gifts
	21. Lean on the Lord	29. Believe
15. Do not worry	22. Miracles	30. Words of faith
16. Silence	23. Peace	31. Seek the Lord
17. Walk close with God	24. Be thankful	
	25. Commitment	

End of month reflections for July 2016

We have a choice in how we respond to others. The best choice is to be kind and faith filled showing your loving heart.

In a complex world, keep your life simple. Praise God in all situations. Listen to Godly counsel. Do what is right and be loyal to God. Have a deep respect for others and show true commitment. Miracles happen when we continuously do good deeds with much love. Trust in the Lord. Be not afraid of the future. Be a helpful person and expect the good to shine in others. Rest in God's peace and do not worry about tomorrow.

When contemplating a decision, remain in silence and listen to the Holy Spirit as you walk close with God. Walk very humbly with your God. He will show you the way. Speak gently with those who are troubled. God will make miracles happen. Be at peace and be thankful. Keep your commitment of faith. Show compassion. There is hope for the future. Accept God's gifts and truly believe in his love. Speak words of faith and always seek the wisdom of the Lord. Let his light shine on your life's journey.

Words for August 2016

1. Friendship
2. Joy
3. Gift of time
4. Spend time with God
5. Child of God
6. Prayer
7. Mercy
8. Divine supply
9. Be trustworthy
10. Believe
11. Peaceful
12. Compassion
13. Acceptance
14. Treasures
15. Quietly wait
16. Rest
17. Jesus
18. Surrender
19. Forgive
20. Pray
21. Kindness
22. Trust
23. Encourage
24. Faithful
25. Believe
26. Peace
27. Guide
28. Service
29. Jesus
30. Support
31. Listen

End of month reflections for August 2016

Friendships increase joy in our lives when we give the gift of time and when we spend more time with God. As a child of God, we lovingly lead a life of prayer. We depend on God's mercy and His divine supply for all our needs.

As God is trustworthy, we are called to believe in his goodness, to live peaceful lives, and to show compassion for the needs of others. Acceptance of God's will in our life create unexpected treasures to flow in and through us as we walk with someone in their pain.

Quietly wait and rest in Jesus's presence as we surrender all to him. As we pray for forgiveness of our sins, we must also forgive others. God's loving kindness is known when we trust in God's mercy. Encourage one another to be faithful. Believe in the peace that will flow in for our well-being.

Let the Holy Spirit be our guide in service to Jesus. We will get the support we need as we listen and respond to his word.

Words for September 2016

1. Seek the Lord
2. Thankfulness
3. Shelter
4. God will supply
5. Friends
6. A loving touch
7. Mercy
8. Walk with God
9. Open heart
10. Transformed
11. Home
12. Values
13. Surrender
14. Spiritual journey
15. Shine
16. Walk in love
17. Persistence
18. Sacrificial love
19. Joy
20. God is good
21. Mercy and compassion
22. Strength
23. Be yourself
24. Pay attention
25. Tenderness
26. Love
27. Gift
28. Lean on God
29. Angels
30. Believing heart

End of month reflections for September 2016

Seek the Lord with all your heart. Have a spirit of thankfulness for the sheltering of God's abundant supply. Friends add a beautiful touch of mercy to our lives. We are to walk with God, keeping our hearts open so our lives will be transformed into his likeness.

Home is a good place to be. Home is to be valued. Surrender all to Jesus on this spiritual journey. Let your light shine by walking in love and humility. Have a spirit of persistence in sacrificial love. Show joy in all we do.

God is good, yes, good all the time. His mercy and compassion gives us strength to be our best self. We need to pay more attention to our own needs and show our self tenderness and love.

Accept the gift of the fact that we can and should lean on God. Accept the gift of the angels' protection. Always keep a believing heart with great love.

Words for October 2016

1. Balance
2. Worship
3. Mercy
4. Listen
5. Beautiful
6. Be a loving presence
7. Care
8. Perseverance
9. Respect
10. Cheerful service
11. Walk with God
12. Faithful
13. Inner Treasure
14. Humble
15. Hope
16. Love
17. A Treasure
18. Peace
19. Holy Spirit
20. Respect
21. Tenderness
22. Faith
23. Unseen Holy Spiritual Forces
24. Overwhelmed by Love
25. Abundant Life
26. Guard
27. Choice
28. Solitude
29. Inspiration
30. Loving Kindness
31. Forgivenesss

End of month reflections for October 2016

To find balance in your life, worship the Lord your God, everyday. His mercy and love will flow through all you do. Listen closely to the beautiful guidance of God's word.

Be a loving presence to all you meet. Let people know that you care deeply. When troubles and trials come, take a stance of perseverance. Respect the difficulties with a cheerful heart. Serve others with a smile by walking with God. It is this faithful service that brings an inner treasure beyond measure.

When you humble yourself before the Lord, you began to have hope for the future. Live in the fullness of God's love. God's love is a real treasure.

Allow God's peace and the Holy Spirit to flow through your very being. Respect the tenderness of your living faith. When you allow all the unseen Holy Spiritual forces to flow, you will be overwhelmed by God's love.

To know and to understand what abundant life is, count the many blessings of your life. Guard your tongue. Your words are your choice. Seek solitude to gain the inspiration you need to show loving kindness and forgiveness.

Words for November 2016

1. Goodness
2. Eternal
3. God's gift
4. Surrender
5. Comfort others
6. Trusted companions
7. God's presence
8. Hold onto God's hand
9. Christ among us
10. Peace
11. Receive
12. Quiet
13. Let go of trying to control
14. Depend on God
15. The love of Christ
16. God's gift of love
17. Holy
18. Have no fear, God is near
19. Encourage
20. Safe
21. Treasures
22. Serve the Lord with a happy heart
23. Silence
24. See the beauty
25. Give Thanks
26. Shelter and protection
27. Devotion
28. Freedom to choose
29. Stillness
30. Mercy

End of month reflections for November 2016

The goodness of God is eternal. God's gift to us, when we surrender our life to him, is the ability to comfort others with the same love we have received. Thank God for the trusted, treasured companions in your life. We sense God's presence in them. As we hold onto God's hand with our family and friends, we know that Christ is among us.

In the stillness of our heart, we come to peace of soul. We receive more comfort when we quiet our busy minds and just let go of trying to control the situations that are beyond our ability. Let God be in charge. Depend on God. The love of Christ is poured out to us through God's gift of love.

Do your best to be a holy person. Have no fear, God is near. God's mercy endures forever. Encourage people to seek the safe place in their life. There are many treasures in life when we serve the Lord with a happy heart.

Silence the distractions by seeing the beauty of the moments listing to the Holy Spirit. Give thanks for the many shelters of protection that devotion to God provides. We have the freedom to choose. Choose what is right.

Words for December 2016

1. Obey
2. Positive
3. Christ with us
4. Treasure
5. Give
6. Kindness
7. Gentleness
8. Be Blessed
9. Encourage
10. Finding
11. Loving Heart
12. Yes Lord
13. Transformed and treasured
14. Miracles
15. Pray
16. Commitment
17. Abundance
18. Loyal
19. Love
20. Spread joy
21. Share the love of Christ
22. Shine
23. Path
24. Knowing God
25. Honor
26. Family and Friends
27. Word Power
28. Blessings
29. Change
30. Keep praying
31. Jesus

End of month reflections for December 2016

Obey the Lord's commands. Take a positive stance in life. Christ is with us. He treasures us. In turn, he wants us to give gentle, loving kindness to each other. We will be blessed by encouraging people. Finding peoples loving hearts by saying yes to the Lord's call will help us to be transformed, treasured souls.

KNOWING GOD IS KNOWING LOVE

 Miracles still happen when we pray. Have a deep commitment to family and friends. Spread the abundance of loyal love and joy for the love of Christ. Let God's love shine on the path you walk.

 Knowing God Is Knowing Love. Honor him by loving deeply. Let God's word and his power continue to be a blessing in each change that comes into your life. Keep praying for Jesus's help. Be a blessing.

Conclusion

We all go through dark days when things just don't seem to be going our way. We feel like God is not with us. But that is just a feeling. Feelings are neither good nor bad. They just are. Our low mood may be caused by a change in our circumstances, something that just happened that was not even our fault. Or it may be because of a sin we committed. The fact remains that God still loves us and as he promised, he is with us. He is compassionate and merciful.

In difficult days (dark nights of the soul), continue to pray. A good prayer is the Divine Mercy prayer:

Eternal God, in whom mercy is endless and the treasury of compassion inexhaustible, look kindly upon us and increase Your mercy in us, that in difficult moments, we might not despair nor become despondent, but with great confidence, submit ourselves to your holy will, which is love and mercy itself. Amen.

There is hope in the darkness. What do you do when you have lost your way and are in darkness? Don't let dark feelings poison your heart. You should tell someone who loves you, so they can pray. You pray too. Even though you feel you can't. Just tell God you are lost in the dark. Tell him you need help in finding your way again. Give yourself to him. Cry! Tears are a healing balm. Tears help wash away the pain. If your friends tell you the truth and the truth hurts, or even if your friends do not understand, realize in your heart that *"wounds from a friend may be accepted as well meant" (Prov. 27:6).*

Our words and actions have consequences. God holds us responsible. Our spiritual life depends on continual conversion. No matter our age, we seek and long for a closer fellowship with God. In troubled time or in sickness, keep our eyes and heart open to God's abiding love.

> *"God is our refuge and strength, an ever present help in trouble. Therefore we will not fear, though the earth gives way and the mountains fall into the heart of the sea, though its waters roar and foam and the mountains quake with surging. The Lord of hosts is with us; our stronghold is the God of Jacob" (Ps. 46:1–3).*

Submit your life to God. He truly loves you. God's love and mercy endures forever. You will come through the darkness to the light of love again. You will be stronger. You can be a help to others because you have been there and survived.

> *"Fear not, I am with you: be not dismayed; I am your God. I will strengthen you and help you, and uphold you with my right hand of justice" (Is. 41:10).*

> *"The darkness is passing and the true light is already shinning" (1 Jn. 2:8).*

> *"For God said, "Let light shine out of darkness, make his light shine in our hearts to give us the light of the knowledge of the glory of God in the face of (Jesus) Christ" (2 Cor. 4:6).*

Be persistent in your prayer life. Prayer does make a difference. Love one another. Love is of God. God is love. Notice on the cover on the front of this book. See how the cross of the Lord stands revealed as the tree of life.

Walk with God on the path of life. Let God be your rock of salvation. God cares for the birds, the flowers, and most of all he cares and loves you. Nothing in life is more awesome than Knowing God's love. Down every road there are blessings to be found in life giving friendships.

> *"Blessed are they who wash their robes so as to have the right to the tree of life and enter the city through its gates" (Rev. 22:14).*

About the Author

Linda Stafford is retired from Tenneco Inc. where she worked in the planning department in Paragould, Arkansas. After forty-two years of dedicated service, she decided to pursue her passion for writing.

Linda was raised General Baptist. She was led by the Holy Spirit to convert to the Catholic faith at age twenty-seven. She enjoys reading and listening to others' faith journey. It is inspiring to see where God places each soul to serve him best.

Linda has been an oblate for Holy Angels Convent in Jonesboro, Arkansas, since 1985.

She loves volunteering at St. Mary's Church and being involved in scripture studies. She was instrumental in setting up the Little Rock Scripture Study program in her parish. She also took time to travel to Louisiana, New Jersey, and around the state of Arkansas to give talks promoting the program and its importance in helping understand and appreciate the Bible.

Linda has one son, Jack. In her spare time, she enjoys reading, reflecting, and spending more time with family and friends. She especially loves creating special treasure hunts for her great nieces and nephews. There are always lots of laughs involving both adults and children.